Through the Look

V

Through the Looking Glass

A Dissenter inside New Labour

LIZ DAVIES

VERSO

London • New York

First published by Verso 2001
© Liz Davies 2001
All rights reserved

Verso
UK: 6 Meard Street, London W1F 0EG
USA: 180 Varick Street, New York, NY 10014–4606
www.versobooks.com

Verso is the imprint of New Left Books

ISBN 1–85984–609–2

British Library Cataloguing in Publication Data
A catalogue record for this book is available from the British Library

Library of Congress Cataloging-in-Publication Data
A catalog record for this book is available from the Library of Congress

Typeset in 10/12½pt ITC New Baskerville by
SetSystems Ltd, Saffron Walden, Essex
Printed by Biddles Ltd, Guildford and King's Lynn

Dedicated to Tony Benn –
for speaking truth to power

Contents

Acknowledgements

Without my election, and those of the other Grassroots Alliance candidates, onto the Labour Party's National Executive Committee, there would be no book. I owe that election to the votes of thousands of Labour Party members and the hard work of many Labour activists up and down the country. They are too numerous to be listed here, but they know who they are.

It was not my intention to write a book when I first stood for election to the NEC. However, I also made it clear from the outset that I had no intention of concealing the events at the NEC: indeed along with the other Grassroots Alliance candidates, I had been elected on a specific commitment to report the votes and discussions at the NEC to Party members. We did so regularly by means of producing a bulletin, which we distributed to constituency Labour parties, and by writing in the left press. During the course of my two-year term on the NEC, it seemed to me that New Labour's twists, turns, machinations and double-speak should be recorded, for posterity and to open up New Labour to scrutiny – by its own members and by the public at large. This book is an attempt to do just that.

Thanks are due to friends and colleagues who either were part of the Grassroots Alliance election campaign and subsequent work on the NEC and National Policy Forum, or helped with this book, or in some cases both. In alphabetical order, they are: Elaine Abbott, Raghip Ahsan, Helen Anderton, Jane Ashworth, Graham Bash, Tony Benn, Ann Black, Jacqui Brown, Bill Butler, Malcolm and Gwyneth Christie, Nick Cohen, Terry Conway, Graham Copp, Jeremy Corbyn, Sarah Cotterill, Irma Critchlow, Tony Dale, Mike

Davies, Ray Davison, Jill Dawn, Vladimir and Vera Derer, Pete Firmin, Jenny Fisher, John Fisher, Celia Foote, Garth and Wendy Frankland, Kath Fry, Alan Goode, Colin Hall, Richard Heffernan, Andy Howell, Solomon Hughes, Cathy Jamieson, Des Kirkland, Suraya Lawrence, Dave Lewney, John Lewis, Leonora Lloyd, Sue Lukes, George McManus, Dorothy Macedo, Hugh MacGrillen (and other comrades at the London Region MSF), Paul Madeley, Ian and Hazel Malcolm-Walker, Judy Maxwell, Amanda Meusz, Lorraine Monk, Anna Monks, Pat and Jim Mortimer, Tim Pendry, Mike Phipps, David Pope, Gary Ransford, Mark Seddon, Christine Shawcroft, Alan Simpson, Dennis Skinner, Dave Statham, Mark Steel, John Stewart, Mark Thomas, Matthew Willgress, Pete Willsman, the late Audrey Wise, Nick Wrack. My parents, Kathleen and Cliff Davies, my brother John and sister-in-law Claire were constantly supportive and tolerant of my lack of free time.

My housing team colleagues at Two Garden Court chambers displayed endless patience as I tried to juggle politics, book-writing and a legal practice. Matthew Jones and Caroline Mitchell managed somehow to ensure that I retained that legal practice, despite all the other commitments. Stephen Simblet and Malek Wan Daud had to overhear endless phone conversations discussing Labour Party politics, and never complained.

Jane Hindle, Sophie Arditti and Pat Harper at Verso did an excellent job turning my manuscript into a book in record time, and Gavin Everall dealt with the marketing.

There are three people without whom this book would not exist. Colin Robinson was a magnificent editor, publisher and friend and a source of constant encouragement. Lachie Stuart patiently sat through endless accounts of New Labour's latest outrages and provided rocklike support, jokes, bridge and fun. Most of all, Mike Marqusee shared with me all the events in this book and had to live with the book being written. Without his support, his encouragement, his writing and cooking skills, his political acuity and his love, I would not have the strength to engage politically as intensively as I do.

Any errors are, of course, my sole responsibility.

Liz Davies, February 2001

Introduction: Enter Stage Left

In October 1998, much to the consternation of Labour Party headquarters at Millbank, I was elected, along with three other leftist dissidents from the Grassroots Alliance, to represent individual Party members on Labour's National Executive Committee. The first meeting of the newly elected NEC was held in Blackpool on the last evening of that year's Party conference. It was a strange experience taking a seat on a body that only three years earlier had ruled that I was unsuitable to stand as a Labour candidate for Parliament.

Although the meeting was formal and perfunctory, attended by both the 1997–98 NEC members and those newly elected, it was tense because the four of us had just won a well-publicised victory over the Millbank machine. It was held at the Stakis, Blackpool's five-star hotel where the great and the good of the Party had been lodged during conference week. I had arranged to meet Cathy Jamieson and Pete Willsman, who had been elected with me on the Grassroots Alliance ticket, at the end of the conference proceedings so that we could find our way to the meeting and make our debut appearances together. But we lost each other somewhere in the vastness of the Winter Gardens and I ended up rushing over to the Stakis on my own. I was nervous that I might be late and even more nervous at the prospect of facing Tony Blair, Clare Short and the like, who had campaigned with ferocity against the Grassroots Alliance and against me in particular.

When I found the room, Pete was sitting outside waiting for me, and we went in together. The meeting had not yet started. The NEC was sitting around a number of tables formed into a large square, with numerous Millbank staffers watching on from the sides. The main focus of the room was the west window, a huge picture window overlooking the Blackpool front and the Irish Sea. It was 5.30pm and there was a perfect and conveniently blinding sunset. The top table, which consisted of the Labour Party Leader Tony Blair, Deputy Leader John Prescott, the outgoing Chair of the Party Richard Rosser, and the outgoing General Secretary Tom Sawyer, was positioned against the west window, and the four men sat with their backs to the setting sun. Facing them, the rest of us could see little but shadowy faces surrounded by bright aureoles. It seemed that Millbank's obsession with stage-management extended even into private meetings of the Party's elected ruling body.

Cathy and Mark Seddon, the fourth member of our newly elected dissident group, had found us four seats together, which immediately faced the top table. NEC members were taking their seats, fetching cups of tea and chatting. Amid an air of rather forced informality, most of the men had taken off their jackets and were in shirtsleeves. Everyone was using first names. Some members of the NEC came up to introduce themselves, shake our hands and congratulate us. In response, I would introduce myself, only to be met with knowing grins. Everyone in the room, most of whom I had never met before, seemed to think they knew exactly who I was and what they thought I represented. The majority of NEC members, and all the Millbank staffers, did their best to ignore our presence, glancing covertly in our direction now and again.

Of course, our very presence at the NEC was a slap in the face for New Labour and Millbank. Many people in the room had campaigned against us, either openly or behind the scenes. Now that we had been elected, we were regarded as uninvited and unwelcome guests. Nobody was quite sure how to react to our presence. Nor were they sure how we would react. I had the distinct impression that, despite our suits, smiles and polite behaviour, most of the room was waiting for us to start unfurling banners or to throw buckets of red paint on the Prime Minister.

As I sat down, the woman sitting next to me, newly elected to the NEC by the trade unions, twisted as far away from me as possible – to the point where it looked like she might fall off her chair. It was as if she feared that even sitting next to me might somehow taint her in Millbank's eyes. Clare Short – Minister for Overseas Development, once a left-winger, now part of the Blair project – was sitting a little further away, looking tense and uncomfortable. In a speech to the 1995 Party conference, she had told the delegates – and thanks to television, the public at large – that I was unfit to represent the Party. Now the Party had rejected her advice. Luckily for both of us, she was leaving the NEC and we would not have to pretend not to notice each other sitting around the same table month in, month out.

Blair began the proceedings by thanking the retiring members of the NEC. He spent some time lauding the contribution of Clare Short and others, but mentioned the left-wing MPs Diane Abbott and Ken Livingstone (neither was present) in the most cursory way. Then the new NEC formally took office. The only item of business was the election of the Chair and Vice-Chair for the coming year. There is a venerable Labour Party convention that dictates that the Vice-Chair from the previous year is unanimously elected as the new Chair. As Party General Secretary, Tom Sawyer assumed the chair for the formal election procedure and asked for nominations. Brenda Etchells, the Vice-Chair and trade union representatve from the AEEU, was immediately nominated and seconded. Sawyer asked if there were any other nominations. All eyes in the room turned to the four of us. It seemed we were considered so unpredictable, so disruptive, that it was feared we would force a pointless contest for the Chair at our first meeting. In truth, it had never occurred to us to nominate anyone – commanding as we did a total of four out of thirty-three votes – and we would have dismissed the idea out of hand had it been suggested. A relieved Tom Sawyer declared Etchells elected in the absence of any other nominations. The meeting was over in twenty minutes, but it had given us all a little taste of the paranoia and pointlessness that were to be the hallmarks of NEC meetings over the next two years.

The NEC meetings were easily the least democratic, most

stitched-up, and most arduously unpleasant meetings I have ever attended, and I have spent many years in political meetings. I joined the Labour Party in 1979, when I was sixteen, filled with excitement at the prospects for socialism, and horror at the dawning reality of Thatcherism. I never confined myself solely to Labour Party activity. I was also an activist in the Campaign for Nuclear Disarmament, the feminist movement and a variety of single-issue campaigns. But since 1979 the Labour Party has been my focus and a part of my identity. Throughout the eighties, I attended meetings, gave out leaflets, went canvassing, organised elections, and held just about every possible office at branch and constituency level. In 1984–85, like every other socialist, I threw myself into support for the miners' strike. In 1990, I was elected as a Labour councillor in Islington and spent the next eight years working to represent one of the most deprived wards in London. During five of those years, I was Chair of the council's women's committee. I was always firmly on the left of the Party, one of many members inspired and sustained by Tony Benn, an unashamed socialist. I was centrally involved in the Labour left magazine *Labour Briefing*, and wrote for other magazines on the left, including *Tribune* and the *Morning Star*.

In 1995, I was catapulted from being an obscure and not atypical Labour Party activist and local councillor to the front pages of the newspapers. In July of that year, I had been democratically selected by Labour Party members in the Leeds North East constituency to be their prospective parliamentary candidate. Usually, if there are no procedural problems with a selection process, the NEC endorses the candidate as a matter of course. But shortly after my selection, the press reported that Blair had "gone ballistic" and that my endorsement would be refused on the grounds that I was too left-wing. A highly public battle over my alleged beliefs and actions then ensued and I found myself on the receiving end of media attention of a scale and nature I had never remotely experienced before. Falsehoods were circulated about my political affiliations and my record as a Labour councillor in Islington, and I was forced to take libel action against three Blairite Islington councillors who concocted a story about me inciting violence at a council meeting. Eventually, I won an apology and accepted payment in lieu of damages as part of a High Court settlement, but that came far too late to have any effect on the fate of my prospective parliamentary candidacy.

Ten weeks after my selection in Leeds, I was interviewed by the NEC's Disputes Committee – for three and a half hours. The NEC as a whole then refused to endorse my selection, but offered no specific reason for the decision. The clear message, however, was that my politics – on the left of the Party – were considered unacceptable under the Blair dispensation. Emergency motions from Leeds North East, Islington North (my local Labour Party) and eleven other constituencies were sent to the 1995 Labour Party Conference protesting at the decision. That was when Clare Short, speaking on behalf of the NEC, had accused me in fairly lurid but entirely unspecific terms of being outside Labour's broad church. A week earlier, I had met Short and asked for her support at the NEC. I had offered to answer any questions she might have about me or my record. She had replied then that she had no particular knowledge of my case or interest in it.

After the NEC's refusal to endorse me, I had remained a member of the Labour Party and a Labour councillor in Islington. Had I genuinely been outside Labour's broad church, I should also, logically, have been removed as a Labour councillor. But the decision on my parliamentary candidacy had never really been about me or my rights. It was widely regarded as an attempt by Blair (who had assumed the Party leadership less than a year before) to send a message: the left would no longer be permitted entry to the Parliamentary Labour Party, and even if they won selections under the new rules (the rules promoted by Blair and his supporters), leftists would not be endorsed. The Party managers were determined to ensure that as many as possible of the new parliamentary intake would be "on message" Blairites, whatever Party members might have preferred.

I may have been the most visible victim of this manoeuvring, but the people who really suffered were the constituency Party members who had selected me. In 1997, long after the press coverage had died down, Leeds North East CLP was suspended by the NEC, and disciplinary proceedings were taken against some of its leading activists, culminating in the expulsion of four of them, including the Chair, Vice-Chair and Treasurer. Their crime was simply that they had defied Millbank and Tony Blair.

It was therefore something of a shock to be sitting at the NEC, but also an honour and a privilege. The four of us had been elected by ordinary Party members, despite Millbank's attempts to paint our election as tantamount to the end of civilisation. We had put ourselves forward to Party members on a platform calling for the redistribution of wealth and power, investment in public services and an end to privatisation, increased taxation of the rich and improved welfare benefits. These ideas may have seemed invidious to Millbank, but they were endorsed by large numbers of Party members. We were also elected to defend Party democracy and the rights of Party activists, and in particular to defend the right to dissent, in opposition to Millbank's control-freak tendency. And we had been elected on a specific commitment to report back to Party members on the events at the NEC – the Party's supreme governing body.

I have served as an elected representative at all levels of the Labour Party and I have always sought to engage with the Party's democratic structures. I have always made it my practice to argue my corner within those structures, and to report debates and decisions back to the Labour Party members whom I represented. As a lawyer, it is second nature to me to work within the rules, and to try to get the best result within the structures given. Of course, I have encountered my share of dirty tricks and dishonest debate, but on the whole it was my experience in the Labour Party that it was possible to engage in open, serious debate and informed decision-making. The meetings may have been frustrating or boring, but they had a purpose, they had political content, and their results could not always be predicted.

I was to find, sadly, that the meetings of the NEC were unlike every other type of labour movement meeting I have attended. Over the next two years, I grew increasingly appalled at the woeful standard of debate and the cynically undemocratic proceedings of the Labour Party's highest decision-making body. The quality of the reports, not to mention the reliability of the information, presented to the NEC by our paid staff (the officials based at Party headquarters at Millbank) would have been considered substandard by most local authority bodies or even voluntary-group management committees. With a few exceptions, NEC members failed to question officials, passively accepted whatever line was being fed them by the leadership, and made no effort to report back to the people who had elected them. Indeed, what the NEC majority, and even more intensely the Millbank officials, most resented about the Grassroots Alliance was that we did report back. I sat at every meeting with notebook and pen, and made no secret that I was recording the proceedings in detail, not for my personal amusement, but as a duty to the people who elected me. We had made a promise to Party members, we stuck to it, and they hated it. I suspect they'll dislike what follows in this book even more.

1

Millbank Trumped

The Labour Party National Executive Committee has a long history as a democratic forum enlivened by hotly contested debates, a kind of larger-than-life political theatre. Readers of Tony Benn's diaries will be familiar with the set-piece, cliffhanger showdowns between left and right, the trade unions and the parliamentary leadership. By the time I was elected in 1998, however, the NEC, like the Party as a whole, had changed.

Traditionally, the section of the NEC elected by the constituency Labour parties was the domain of the left, and when it linked with discontented trade union representatives on the NEC in the seventies and early eighties, it was a formidable force for Labour leaders to contend with. But after 1985, in the grip of what was originally dubbed "New Realism", the unions had shifted to the right and confined criticism of the Party leadership or of Party policy to stage whispers and backdoor lobbying. At the same time, more and more MPs loyal to the leadership had come to be elected to the constituency section at the expense of left-wing rebels. By 1989 only Tony Benn and Dennis Skinner remained to speak for the left in the Party. Each depended on the other to second motions, and their motions were routinely defeated by overwhelming majorities. In 1993, Tony Benn found himself the sole left member of the NEC, with nobody to second his motions.

In 1994, election of the constituency section of the NEC by all Party members using one member, one vote was introduced. Under this system, designed to keep out the left, Dennis Skinner and Diane Abbott won seats in 1994 and retained their places each year thereafter. In 1997 Ken Livingstone beat Peter Mandelson to take the complement up to three left-wingers. However, at the same conference in October 1997 that saw Livingstone elected, the rules were changed in yet another attempt by the leadership to rid the NEC of the left once and for all.

The proposals contained in the NEC document "Partnership in Power" had been launched just before the 1997 general election and were approved at Conference in the wake of Labour's landslide. The Party's decision-making structures were changed to take effect from 1998. No longer could constituency parties or trade unions put motions directly to Conference. Instead policy making was supposed to occur, by "consensus", through a body called the National Policy Forum. Debates about policy would be held behind closed doors, and Conference would be used instead to project the Party's image to the public. The NEC saw its membership restructured. The twelve trade union representatives would remain, elected by the trade unions. However, the seven constituency seats would be reduced to six, and MPs would no longer be eligible to stand in that section. New sections were created: the Parliamentary Labour Party would elect three seats, and there would be two seats elected by Labour councillors. The five reserved women's seats were abolished, and instead at least half of the seats in each section had to be held by women. The remainder of the NEC consisted of a representative from Young Labour, one from the socialist societies (including the Co-Operative Party, Socialist Education Association and other societies affiliated to the Labour Party), the Leader, Deputy Leader and Treasurer of the Party, the Leader of the European Parliamentary Labour Party, and three members appointed directly by the government (or the shadow cabinet when Labour is in opposition). These different sections – trade unions, constituencies, PLP, councillors, Young Labour, socialist societies and government – were defined by the "Partnership in Power" document as the Labour Party's "stakeholders", and the new 33-strong NEC was supposed to embrace them all.

The creation of sections for the PLP and Labour councillors meant that those seats could only be held by professional Labour

Party politicians, likely to be responsive to the wishes of the leadership. The government places were, of course, directly nominated by Blair. The trade union representatives owed their seats to their various general secretaries. Of the entire NEC, only the six constituency representatives plus the Treasurer were elected by the membership as a whole.

Millbank's thinking was that under the new rules the left would be unlikely to win any of the constituency seats, since in the absence of MPs it would lack the clout and recognition of the "big names" (Skinner, Abbott, Livingstone) needed to win one member, one vote contests in the Labour Party. There was a general view, held by both supporters and opponents of "Partnership in Power", that the elections for the constituency section would no longer be a left–right battleground and that those seats would effectively be in Millbank's gift.

Diverting policy making through the National Policy Forum, rather than Conference, also meant a downgrading of the role of the NEC. It had previously been responsible for policy between each annual conference. Now, it was no longer to discuss policy at all, confining itself to decisions over the Party's administration. However, since NEC meetings usually began with a report from the Party leader, and then questions to him, it was inevitable that policy matters would be raised. In addition, the NEC retained the power to supervise (or block) the selection of parliamentary candidates, to oversee Party finances and to make a wide range of organisational decisions with major implications for ordinary Party members. Reflecting the apparent downgrading of its status, the NEC would meet once every two months, rather than monthly as previously. Most Party business would be conducted through its sub-committees: Organisation, Finance, Development, Local Government, and Women.

Nonetheless, the NEC remained, formally, Labour's supreme governing body between annual conferences, with responsibility for election campaigns, Party management, and Party finances. It also retained its symbolic importance as the principal sounding board for Party opinion. Despite the various changes, its membership and its proceedings were still matters of considerable concern to the Party managers. For them, the NEC remained a source of potential embarrassment.

I did not attend Party Conference in October 1997 but I remember seeing an *Evening Standard* headline reporting that Livingstone had defeated Mandelson. I found myself punching the air in delight. Soon after that, I was asked in various emails and telephone calls whether I would consider standing for the constituency section in 1998 under the new rules.

I was bound to be a controversial candidate, whatever I said or did. Given the events in 1995, I had some name recognition among Party members, but it was an ambiguous one. Depending on whom you spoke to, I was either the woman who had been badly treated by Blair and robbed of an opportunity to stand for Parliament, or I was the nightmare figure whose views were said to be beyond the pale.

Early in 1998, there were informal meetings in London among groups on the left and centre of the Labour Party who had worked together to oppose "Partnership in Power" the previous year. We had not succeeded then, but we had found that in opposing Blairism, we could work effectively together. We had priorities in common: we were opposed to Millbank's control-freakery, we wanted to defend Party democracy and create a transparent policy-making process. We also had broader political values in common: commitments to redistribution of wealth, and to defence and extension of trade union rights and public services, and opposition to privatisation – all beliefs not shared by the Blairites but held, we were convinced, by large numbers of Party members. Having lost the battle to oppose "Partnership in Power", we decided to seize the moment and put together a united centre–left slate to contest the 1998 NEC constituency section elections.

The slate that emerged was a credible one. The six of us who stood for the Centre–Left Grassroots Alliance all had long records as Party activists and were relatively well known to Party members. And we had a unique opportunity. All the constituency seats for many years had been filled by MPs. Since they were now ineligible to stand, there were no incumbents fighting the election. All six seats really were up for grabs.

The slate was balanced between the centre and the left, between men and women (a requirement since three of the six seats had to be held by women), and regionally. I already knew Mark Seddon, Pete Willsman and Christine Shawcroft. I met Andy Howell and Cathy Jamieson during the election campaign.

Mark had been the editor of *Tribune* since 1994 and a member of the Labour Party from the age of fifteen. *Tribune* in the late 1980s had wandered far from its traditional left critique of the leadership, but in the 1990s it regained its reputation as a paper prepared to speak truth to power. Mark's editorials had blasted Blair and New Labour for sticking to Tory public spending plans, for failing to redistribute wealth, and for their assault on Party democracy.

Pete Willsman was a long-standing Party activist, a key member of the Campaign for Labour Party Democracy since the 1970s. From 1981 to 1994, he had been elected annually by constituency delegates onto the powerful Conference Arrangements Committee – a job he revelled in. Pete is a master of procedural and technical detail and knows the rule book and the precedents back to front. He was hugely popular with conference delegates, reporting at fringe meetings and through bulletins on the procedural manipulations of the Conference Arrangements Committee. After he lost his seat on the CAC in 1994, he was elected the following year by a one member, one vote ballot of Party members to the National Constitutional Committee – the Party's disciplinary committee – and there he tried his best to prevent expulsions and disciplinary action against left-wingers. Having sat on two key Party committees, and having been around since the late 1970s, Pete already knew most of the major players in the Party and, despite his rocklike socialist commitments, managed to keep on reasonable terms with most of them. Over the years, his broad Hampshire accent and charming grin have been deployed to defuse many a personal or political attack.

Christine Shawcroft had been a Labour councillor in Tower Hamlets in London's East End for twelve years. Like Pete, she had been a familiar figure on the left of the Party for some time, and had served on the London Labour Party executive. Under the old rules, she had stood several times for the NEC women's section and secured a respectable vote from Party members in a contest entirely determined by a handful of trade union executives. As part of New Labour's iron grip on the Party, prospective council candidates now have to be vetted by a selection panel before they are allowed even to put their names forward to local Party members for selection. Despite Christine's record as an effective and successful local councillor who had consistently increased the Labour vote in her area, her left-wing views made her unacceptable to the Blairites on her local selection panel and she was deprived of the opportunity to seek re-election for the council in 1998.

Andy Howell was the Chair of Labour Reform, which had been formed in 1997 in order to oppose "Partnership in Power", and was made up of Party activists who did not regard themselves as being on the left, but were still strongly opposed to the leadership's attacks on Party democracy. Despite a history of mistrust, they had struck up a working alliance with the left in order to oppose "Partnership in Power" and, in the course of that campaign, we had all found that there was increasing agreement between the left and the centre on the need to oppose New Labour policies and practices. Labour Party politics were in Andy's blood. His father (who sadly died in 1998) was Dennis Howell MP, the much-admired Minister for Sport in the 1974–79 Labour government. Andy was a councillor in Birmingham and, until New Labour came along, was firmly on the right of the Party and opposed to the left. But like Roy Hattersley, Andy suddenly found that he had more in common with the left than with New Labour.

Cathy Jamieson is now a member of the Scottish Parliament and the Deputy Leader of the Scottish Labour Party, but in 1998 she was the sole left-wing member of the Party's Scottish Executive. She had a strong reputation in Scotland, not least because she would regularly send out a newsletter detailing the debates and decisions of the Scottish Executive to local parties. Although the six of us never actually met in one room either during or after the campaign, we forged a strong and trusting relationship.

I was immensely impressed, later in the summer, when all our candidates rallied round the slate, rebutting a stream of personal attacks and resisting attempts to divide us.

Like the slate itself, the name Centre–Left Grassroots Alliance emerged through a process of meetings, phone calls and emails. "Centre–Left" was, obviously, an attempt to sum up the political breadth of the alliance. "Grassroots Alliance" was the brainchild of Tim Pendry, one of the initiators of Labour Reform, who was to become the press spokesperson for the Grassroots Alliance. It turned out to be a catchy name, one that Party members could identify with, and that drew a clear distinction between ourselves and the candidates supported by the leadership.

In early 1998, less than a year after the long-awaited general election victory, there were already mutterings of discontent among Party members. Nobody expected miracles from Blair's government. We all understood that the legacy of eighteen years of Tory rule could not be swept away overnight and, in any case, Blair's manifesto had gone out of its way to dampen down expectations. But Party members had been shocked by the Ecclestone affair – New Labour's first public brush with sleaze – and by the cuts in lone parent benefit. Members might not have expected radical change in the short run, but nor had they expected to see a Labour government in hock to millionaires or taking a punitive approach to single parents. The low level of the minimum wage was also a disappointment. On top of that, Party members all around Britain were feeling the brunt of Millbank's control-freakery. Long-standing councillors were finding themselves prevented by Party officials from putting their names forward for reselection as Labour candidates. There were rumours that the panel of candidates for the Scottish Parliament and the Welsh Assembly would be tightly controlled by Party officials, and that the list system for the European elections in 1999 would mean that any MEP who had displeased Blair would face the chop.

Amid this atmosphere of muted but growing dissent, leaflets for the Grassroots Alliance were sent out in April to constituency parties, and we started campaigning for nominations. Previously, the MPs standing for the constituency section had only needed

the nomination of their own constituency Party. Now we each
needed at least three nominations: one from our own constituency Party plus two others. What's more, the three nominations
had to come from constituency parties in three different regions.
This was yet another hurdle introduced by Millbank to make
standing for election more difficult, and to deter candidates who
did not have the assistance of the Millbank machine.

But Millbank were taken by surprise. Nobody at headquarters
had anticipated that there would be a single organised centre–left
slate, or that it would contain names that were familiar to Party
members. Millbank itself had not yet put a slate together. Assum-
ing that the constituency seats could not now be won by left-
wingers, they had been content to sit back and offer gentle
encouragement to any New Labour supporter who wanted to put
his or her name forward. Initially, it appeared they would end up
fielding more than six candidates for the six places. But once they
realised that the Grassroots Alliance was potentially a serious
threat, they began to panic. On 3 May 1998, Paul Routledge in
the *Independent on Sunday* reported the formation of our slate and
that Millbank and staffers from the Downing Street political unit
had been meeting to draw up a campaign against us. Millbank's
strategy was reported to be to encourage celebrity "luvvies" –
Michael Cashman was named – to stand against us. Michael
Cashman is now a Labour MEP, but at that time was principally
known for having been in *EastEnders* for three years. A Number
Ten staffer was said to have been put in charge of the NEC
campaign. On 24 May 1998, *Scotland on Sunday* quoted an anonymous Party official as saying, "Blair's people have completely gone
to sleep on this. The left slate is well organised and is picking up
nominations across the country."

When nominations closed on 9 June, all six of us had achieved
far more than the three constituency nominations we each
needed. Between us, we had 128 nominations (out of over 600
constituency Labour parties) and we were all going to be on the
ballot paper. In total, twenty candidates had received the requisite
number of nominations. It was still not clear who Millbank's
favoured candidates would be, and there were far more Blairites

nominated than there were seats available. Belatedly, Millbank flexed its muscles. Within a few days of the close of nominations, and before the election statements or ballot papers had been printed, three Blairites had withdrawn. Two others withdrew after the ballot paper had been printed, so that their names appeared in the election statement against the stamp "withdrawn". That left a Millbank slate of six: Michael Cashman, Diana Jeuda, Margaret Payne, Rita Stringfellow, Terry Thomas and Sylvia Tudhope, as well as three non-aligned candidates. On 3 August 1998, the *Guardian* reported: "Downing St slims NEC slate to keep out left"; it referred to the slate backed by Downing Street and Millbank as a "Members First" slate, a not very convincing riposte to our Grassroots Alliance.

Of the six, the two strongest candidates were Michael Cashman and Diana Jeuda. Cashman had his fame as a soap opera star to cash in on, and he had also served as a spokesperson for Stonewall, the gay rights organisation. Jeuda had been a long-standing member of the NEC in the trade union section as a representative of USDAW, the shop-workers' union. She had recently retired as an USDAW employee and was seeking another means of getting on the NEC. In the past, she had had something of a reputation as a member of "the soft left" – a concept that no longer applies in a Labour Party fundamentally divided between New Labour and everyone else. Her reputation for being relatively independent-minded was tarnished by her agreeing to stand as part of the Millbank "Members First" slate. Roy Hattersley described her in the *Guardian* as mildly eccentric and prone to passing time in committee meetings by splicing rope ends. The Members First slate were aware that being too closely associated with the leadership was not a vote winner. They described themselves as being prepared to be critical, but only behind closed doors. In my two years on the NEC, I never saw Cashman utter a word of criticism on either side of a closed door, and although Jeuda would sometimes express guarded criticisms, she never failed to vote according to the leadership's wishes, save for one final act of symbolic rebellion at her (and my) very last NEC meeting.

Between May and July 1998, I travelled Britain speaking at meetings organised by local Labour left-wingers. We found that the meetings attracted a wider turnout than expected and that our platform of democracy in the Labour Party, commitment to redistribution of wealth, proper funding for public services and opposition to discrimination was well received by Party members. We distributed leaflets as widely as possible and spoke to as many Party members as we could contact. *Tribune*, *Labour Left Briefing* and the *Morning Star* reported our campaign and carried regular articles by the candidates. The campaign for the Millbank slate, in contrast, was invisible on the ground.

On 10 August 1998, a *Guardian* editorial called for "a vote for Labour diversity" and urged Party members to vote for us. It called us "proudly off-message", whilst carefully stating that it would have differences with each of us. This editorial threw Millbank into a frenzy. Over the next few days Blairites deluged the *Guardian* letters page. Supporters of the Grassroots Alliance responded and the letters page became a battleground. Suddenly, the campaign was receiving press attention. This was what Millbank had wanted to avoid, but once it started to happen, they used all their clout to ensure that they won the media war, as I was to discover on 13 August 1998.

Ballot papers had arrived through Party members' letterboxes that morning. The ballot paper gave members a choice of how to vote: by post or by telephone. It had not been announced in advance that telephone voting would be used, and the NEC, meeting at the end of July, had never given approval in any form for the practice, for which there was no precedent in the Party. I received a message that Pete Willsman was asking all of us to write to the General Secretary querying the use of telephone voting. He and Christine had, apparently, already written. I therefore faxed a letter to the General Secretary, Tom Sawyer, asking when the decision had been made and what procedures there were in place to prevent any abuse.

Three hours later, all hell broke loose as the press phoned to tell me that Tom Sawyer had issued a media release accusing me of a concerted campaign of slur and innuendo against Labour

Party staff. I was asked to debate with Sawyer on the BBC Radio *Today* programme, but refused – after all, Sawyer was the Party's General Secretary, the returning officer for the election in which I was now a candidate, and responsible for its fair conduct. The next morning, I woke up to hear Sawyer debating with Ken Livingstone on the *Today* programme. Sawyer complained that whenever the Party came into contact with me, I wrote them letters. It was easy for Livingstone to demolish Sawyer's flimsy pretext for issuing a public attack on me – reminding listeners that Millbank's foot soldiers had already been required to apologise to me in the High Court for a previous attack – and I did wonder just why Sawyer allowed himself to be used for such undignified dirty work. For the next few days, the press reported the row, together with the first predictions that the left might actually win some of the NEC seats. Millbank and Downing Street were said to be in a panic.

The media war did not let up. On 18 August 1998, on the bus on my way to work, I opened the *Independent* to find columnist David Aaronovitch claiming that "the Trots are back with a vengeance" with particular reference to me. In a display of the tortuous logic of guilt by association that would have made Joe McCarthy blanch, Aaronovitch managed to insinuate that I was in some way connected to the IRA and even the horrific Omagh bombing. "Trot", of course, has long been New Labour's favourite term of abuse, applied to all left-wing dissenters, regardless of their actual ideological convictions or political affiliations. As it happens, I am not a Trotskyist. In 1998, as in 1995, I found myself constantly writing to the newspapers to correct this allegation – which, as any Trotskyist will tell you, is absurd. In 1998, as in 1995, however, the very assertion that I was not a Trotskyist was twisted by Blairites into an apparent admission. "She vehemently denies that she is a Trotskyist but as the aim of such people is to infiltrate political organisations by stealth and destroy them from within, that is a bit like insisting that you are not a spy or a user of prostitutes," wrote Sîon Simon in the *Spectator*. Just how do you answer that chain of argument?

On 10 September 1998, both the *Guardian* and the *Independent* reported that the Grassroots Alliance would win four out of the six seats, and named the six likely to top the poll. Voting was still open – the ballot did not close until 25 September – but the prediction proved uncannily accurate. At the time, I dismissed all media reports as spin and refused to believe any predictions. In hindsight, the reports were so accurate that there must have been a leak – to Millbank and then on to the media – from inside Unity Security Balloting Ltd, the organisation conducting the ballot.

In the meantime, the Members First slate was spending hundreds of thousands of pounds campaigning against us. It bought three half-page adverts in Sunday newspapers at a cost of at least £40,000 each. In many constituencies represented by New Labour MPs, every Party member received a personal letter from their MP recommending the Members First slate. Strangely, the wording of all of these letters was identical – no matter which MP was sending them out. On top of that, somebody had employed a telephone canvassing company to ring Party members to try to persuade them to vote for the Members First slate. On 16 September 1998, the *Guardian* asked how the telephone canvassers had obtained the Party membership list, and how much the operation had cost. It further reported in detail a phone call from the company to a Party member (they had made the mistake of phoning my old friend Jacqui Brown) in which the company had said that "the Party" wanted her to vote for the Members First slate. Members First was said to be bankrolled by the AEEU, but that did not explain its access to the Labour Party membership list.

In contrast, we had no access to the Party's membership list, and spent in total around £3,000 on our campaign. We relied on volunteer Party members around the country to distribute leaflets and organise meetings for us. Although a *Guardian* editorial had called for a vote for us, far more inches of newsprint in both the *Guardian* and the *Independent* had been devoted to attacking us, both personally and politically. Some of the attacks were particularly risible: Tom Sawyer, a leading NUPE official during the 1978 Winter of Discontent, managed to suggest that Mark and I had been responsible for bringing down the 1979 Labour government – presumably in between doing our O levels.

In a last, desperate attempt to stop us, Millbank went on the offensive on 18 September 1998 – one week before the ballot closed – with an extraordinary diatribe by Neil Kinnock in the *Guardian*. Kinnock's attack was the most personal yet. He accused me and other contributors to *Labour Left Briefing* of engaging in "politics with a perpetual sneer" and of "sour sectarianism". He accused Mark Seddon of being a dupe of the left. Apparently trying to compensate for its editorial endorsement of the Grass-roots Alliance and to restore good relations with Millbank, the *Guardian* not only ran Kinnock's article in its comment section but also turned its publication into a front-page story under the headline "Kinnock lays into hard left 'plotters'". The front-page story simply rehashed Kinnock's splenetic accusations, without any comment or balancing quotes or material from us or our supporters. Mike White, the journalist who wrote the story, later tried to claim to me that he had attempted to contact me for a comment. This was simply not true. I was at home on the evening of 17 September 1998, and in any case I have an answering machine. About 10.30pm, Mark rang me to say that he had heard that there was an attack on us by Neil Kinnock. At about midnight, the Press Association rang me for a comment and faxed the article through to me. I gave them a comment, and then endured a sleepless, anxious night. It is not a pleasant experience to read such vitriol directed at you, and know that the following morning thousands of *Guardian* readers, who know nothing about you, will also be reading it.

I spent most of the next day trying to persuade the *Guardian* to grant us some kind of right of reply. In the end, the only reply they would permit to the extended (and woefully inaccurate) attacks they had printed so extensively on their front and inside pages were two brief letters from Mark and myself, trying to set the record straight. But in his *Guardian* column on 23 September, Mark Steel took on Neil Kinnock with aplomb: "part of his attack on the candidates of the Grassroots Alliance is that they were to blame for Labour losing elections. This is like David Batty saying the reason we were knocked out of the world cup was because Liz Davies can't take penalties."

By the time Party Conference came around, I felt as though nothing could be predicted. I believed none of the speculations in the press. All I knew was that the election campaign was now over and I was relieved. I had always assumed that Millbank's grip over the Party, and its capacity to spin the media and engage in dirty tricks, would be sufficient to prevent our election. At the outset of the campaign, it had seemed to me that the Grassroots Alliance would have done well if its candidates came in as close runners-up. After all, with the exception of Livingstone's victory over Mandelson the previous year, up till this time Blair had pretty much got everything and anything he had wanted from Party members. Now, it was clear that all bets were off.

Conference started on Sunday, 27 September, with the NEC results announcement timetabled for Wednesday. Early on Sunday morning, as I walked along Blackpool front at 6.15am for a radio interview, Wednesday seemed a long time ahead. I found myself wishing that it would come sooner and that this whole ordeal would all be over. The last time I had been to Conference was in 1995 when I was treated like a pariah, and at one point was chased around the conference centre by a media pack that seemed crazed by the scent of blood. When I agreed to become a candidate for the NEC, I had steeled myself for a repeat performance, but I wasn't looking forward to it. I spent that Sunday morning being interviewed by the media and attending the Campaign for Labour Party Democracy pre-conference rally, traditionally the conference week's first gathering of the left. At the CLPD rally, there was a rumour going around that the results would be announced that afternoon in Conference. I phoned Mark Seddon (who was at home, having planned to travel up on Monday) and his immediate reaction was that bringing forward the announcement must mean that we had won. Blair was scheduled to address the troops on Tuesday, and it would be crazy indeed to spoil his moment in the limelight with this nasty and unexpected business of the Grassroots Alliance.

When I went into Conference for the announcement, I found that my designated seat was at the back of the hall behind a pillar.

The other Islington North delegate was seated next to me, and at least not actually behind the pillar. As we were going into Conference, it became obvious that the press had already heard rumours. They told me that the Grassroots Alliance had won four out of the six seats.

Christine Shawcroft and I sat in Conference together, waiting for the results. We were surrounded by photographers, who were so intrusive to other conference delegates that we had to move to the end of a row to minimise the disturbance. The results were read out to Conference amid a strange silence. Mark had topped the poll (with 75,584 votes), followed by Michael Cashman (70,256 votes), Diana Jeuda (62,509), myself (61,970), Cathy (61,707) and Pete (58,108)– just as the leaks in the *Guardian* and *Independent* had predicted for some weeks. A minority of the constituency delegates cheered and clapped, but most of the hall was silent. These days, conference delegates are much more Blairite than grassroots Party members as a whole – and we had been elected by a vote of the latter, and not the former. In addition, it should be remembered that at New Labour's conferences, elected delegates are massively outnumbered by lobbyists, wannabee-MPs, and representatives of big business, none of whom were inclined to applaud our victory. Christine, Cathy and I gave a statement to the press saying that Party members had not been put off by the smears and abuse, that they had voted for redistribution of wealth and power and for democracy and diversity in the Party. The press then left us alone.

An hour or so later I left Conference and found my friends waiting outside in the street, celebrating the victory so many people had worked so hard for. In our celebrations we joined demonstrators marching against cuts in public services. Tony Benn was speaking to the rally at the end of the demonstration and we set off to find him. As I walked towards the rally, various people leaving it recognised me and congratulated me. When I found Tony Benn he gave me a huge hug. My friends from Leeds North East constituency, who had been expelled by New Labour for the crime of having selected me as their prospective parliamentary candidate, were also there and were all ecstatic. It's rare

for ordinary people without money or media friends to be able to
turn the tables on the likes of Millbank, and I think an awful lot
of people got a very big kick out of our success.

The result was greeted by the press as a warning to Blair and a
triumph for the left. Millbank, of course, played it down by
pointing out that the four of us made no difference whatsoever
to the outcome of any of the votes at the 33-strong NEC and that
the Party's policies would not change. There were no potential
troublemakers in any of the other sections of the new-look NEC.
The twelve trade union representatives would all do their general
secretaries' bidding. The Parliamentary Labour Party had voted
(in a recorded vote, not a secret ballot) for three leadership
loyalists: Clive Soley, Chair of the PLP, Anne Begg MP and Pauline
Green MEP, rejecting Dennis Skinner. The councillors had
returned two loyalists: Sally Powell and Jeremy Beecham. Blair
had appointed Mo Mowlam, Ian McCartney and Hilary Armstrong
to the "government" places. The votes at the NEC were not going
to be close.

I spent the rest of the week in Conference as a delegate from
Islington North. Suddenly the pressure from the press had come
off and I felt like a human being again, not under scrutiny the
entire time. The left was buoyed up for the whole of Conference
and cheered all the Grassroots Alliance candidates when we spoke
at fringe meetings. (Even though we were delegates to Conference, somehow none of us managed to catch the Chair's eye
when we wanted to speak.) Meanwhile, the four of us, Mark,
Cathy, Pete and I, were wondering just how to engage with an
NEC whose other members clearly regarded us as unwelcome
intruders.

2

The Bermuda Triangle

Why did I stand for the National Executive Committee? First, because I wanted to help ensure that Labour Party members were given a real choice in the elections under the new rules. Second, because I wanted to provide Party members with a voice in the Party's highest body. I was aware that the NEC had changed since Tony Benn's days, but I hoped to be able, at least, to report to Party members about the decisions being made in their names, and to be able to express at the NEC, and through the NEC to a larger public, the concerns and priorities of the Party members who had voted for me. All four of us hoped that, with the mandate of a substantial vote of Party members behind us, we would be able to pose serious questions and receive serious answers from Party officials. We looked forward to engaging in what we knew would be a difficult debate, but at least, thanks to our election, there would be debates, and even votes.

But it soon became clear that Millbank's conception of the role of the NEC was an entirely different one. On 27 October, an "away-day" for the new NEC – supposedly a time for strategic thinking and open-ended discussion – was organised by Party officials at Congress House, the TUC headquarters. The orginal invitation had said that the venue would be 10 Downing Street, which seemed to me to be dangerously blurring the lines between government and Party. I assume that's why the venue was eventually moved to Congress House.

We were seated around the room in alphabetical order, which placed me between Michael Cashman and Alan Donnelly MEP, leader of the European Parliament Labour Party. I noticed that, as at Conference, people were very uncomfortable with our presence. Alan Donnelly seemed a little shocked when I offered to get him a cup of coffee as I was getting one for myself. Neither Blair nor Prescott was present.

Margaret McDonagh, the Party's newly appointed General Secretary, and David Pitt-Watson, the finance director, were running the away-day. There was much emphasis on overhead projectors and flipcharts and much use of management consultancy jargon. There were charts with titles such as "strategic transformation: visualise". The most bizarre was one headed "Our Bermuda Triangle", containing three boxes labelled "people", "Party", and "government", and three lines linking the boxes. It was never explained to us why this three-way relationship should be dubbed a "Bermuda triangle". Did Millbank fear that Labour would somehow disappear into thin air while negotiating these (dangerous) democratic currents?

This was the first time I had seen Margaret McDonagh close-up, though I had encountered her in passing when she was a regional officer at the London Labour Party. She had started her career in the labour movement as an organiser for the EETPU, working for Frank Chapple, the notorious right-winger, and it was there that she received her initial training in fixing the left. She moved on to the London Labour Party in the late 1980s; here it seemed as though her only responsibility was to keep tabs on Party dissidents. She is still remembered in London for attending constituency Party meetings and assiduously writing down the names of all the members who gave left-wing speeches. In 1996 she had become Assistant General Secretary of the national Labour Party. As soon as she was appointed, she was being talked about as the next General Secretary. In 1998 Tom Sawyer retired to the House of Lords and McDonagh duly succeeded him. The away-day was her first NEC meeting as General Secretary.

If appearances were all, McDonagh would be a refreshing contrast to the middle-aged men in grey suits who have provided the public face of the Labour Party for so many decades: the first woman General Secretary of the Party, in her late thirties, with blonde hair, dressed professionally and stylishly. But McDonagh is utterly single-minded, and her preoccupation with fixing all proceedings at every level on behalf of the New Labour project is her most – indeed, her only – discernible characteristic. She is known to work long hours and expects the rest of the Millbank staff to do the same. There have been complaints about her dictatorial attitude towards the staff; all the management team working with Sawyer have left since McDonagh was appointed. Nobody knows whether she has interests outside the Labour Party. Stories abound that McDonagh is so obsessed with it that her way of relaxing is to pop out on a Sunday morning and get in a few hours' leafleting.

I am sure that she is capable of being perfectly friendly to people whom she likes, or who are useful to her. She had no use whatsoever for the Grassroots Alliance and was not going to expend any energy in any sort of false friendliness. She would say the minimum pleasantry – "How are you?" – if it was unavoidable, but that would be it. She and I were both delighted just to be able to nod at each other, and not engage in a pretence of friendship. She had a rather different relationship with Pete, who could charm a viper, or at least is always willing to have a try! It should be said that this relationship never stopped McDonagh being directly rude to Pete at meetings; in fact, she was probably ruder to Pete than to the rest of us, but she would sometimes swap a joke with him. Even then, the necessity of prosecuting the Blairite agenda always prevailed. However much McDonagh may have joked with Pete, she never let slip a single indiscretion unless she intended to.

With McDonagh in charge, there is not even the pretence of even-handedness within NEC meetings. She intervenes constantly in the discussion (despite being a member of staff, not an elected member of the NEC) in order to reinforce the New Labour line. She will slip in controversial proposals buried away in the detail of a paper that is not laid before members of the NEC until the meeting, and then not refer to those proposals at all when introducing the paper, in the hope that no one will notice them. At NEC meetings we were exhorted time and time again to save the time of the meeting by raising detailed concerns directly with the General Secretary. I started off my term of office by trying to do exactly that. I repeatedly wrote directly to McDonagh only to find both that it took three chasing letters before I even received an acknowledgement from her, and that never, ever would I receive a substantive answer to a serious and specific question. I soon gave up this one-sided correspondence.

The Party finance director, Pitt-Watson, came from a background of management consultancy, and was keen on the tools of the trade: flipcharts, Powerpoint presentations, etcetera. With a soft Scottish accent, he would make a point of appearing inclusive and seemed to distance himself from the usual approach of Labour Party staff, which was to behave as though the Grassroots Alliance either did not or had no right to exist. Underneath, however, he was as factional and sectarian as the others. His approach was to suggest that, if we behaved in what he called a "less confrontational" way, we might be listened to with respect. We quickly discovered that, however we behaved, we were listened to with no respect whatsoever, and that Pitt-Watson's little homilies were just attempts to diffuse whatever points we were trying to make. He was playing the "soft cop" to the others' "hard cop", but he was too easy to see through.

Two themes quickly emerged at the away-day. The first was that the principal role of the NEC was, it now appeared, solely to give public support to the government. In a workshop, Michael Cashman announced dramatically, "Our role is to proselytise to Party members", and then sat back as though he had just delivered a line of scripted dialogue. He seemed very tense and ready to explode in hostility the moment anyone had the temerity to disagree with him. When I used the dreaded word "accountability", Cashman accused me of "Stalinism" and Margaret Prosser, the TGWU official and Party Treasurer, also flared up, saying that we could not possibly attempt to hold the government accountable to the NEC. I insisted that the role of the NEC was to let the government know what Party members were concerned about. That was what I had been elected to do.

Underlying the theme of supporting the government was an

insidious mistrust of Party members. There were constant complaints that "difficult" Party members were criticising the government. Sarah Ward, representing Young Labour on the NEC,
suggested that this was because Party members had got used to
attacking the government when Labour was in opposition and
"old habits die hard". Another explanation put forward was that
Millbank had failed to deliver its message to Party members and
that this could be solved by a technical fix. I said that the
government was criticised over lone parent benefit because its
decision had been wrong, not because of any failure of communi-
cation. Sarah Ward came up with the idea that there should be
somebody on each constituency general committee whose job
it was to defend the government. Most of the others seemed
to think that this was a good idea. I had visions of political
commissars.

At lunchtime, I was standing outside Congress House with Mark
and Sally Powell, who represented Labour councillors on the
NEC, when John Prescott's car drew up. I had never met him
before. He wandered over to us and started chatting amiably,
asking how the morning had gone. I found myself rather nervous:
here was the Deputy Prime Minister gossiping informally. He was
saying that he was late because he had been defending Alan
Meale MP, his parliamentary private secretary. Two days previously, the papers had been full of stories about Meale lobbying
ministers in Prescott's department over a planning inquiry on
behalf of a wealthy Cypriot businessman. Prescott said jovially,
"We don't want to hang Alan Meale out to dry," and then, patting
me on the arm and smiling, added, "It's you that we want to hang
out to dry!" I was taken aback, but managed to stammer out
"Good to meet you, too, John," in reply.

In the afternoon, Prescott spoke to the meeting. I was struck by
how clear and concise he was and how unlike his popular image.
At the NEC, he spoke in properly formed sentences, did not
succumb to malapropisms, and made all his points in a logical
order. He came over as someone who had spent a lifetime
operating in labour movement meetings and knew exactly what
he was doing at every stage in the proceedings.

Then McDonagh took over and Millbank's second grievance, after dissident members, was aired extensively: the media and its alleged hostility to the New Labour government. The most troublesome forces were said to be the *Guardian* and *Newsnight*. McDonagh complained that New Labour had had "a bad summer" in the media, citing in particular how Tom Sawyer had been asked to go on the *Today* show only to find himself debating against Ken Livingstone. What she was urging on NEC members was the effective centralisation of all press relations. Diana Jeuda spoke first, saying that it was a difficult thing for her to say, but that she would reserve the right to decide what she would tell the media. I agreed with her. I referred to the *Today* programme and pointed out that Sawyer was originally booked to debate with me, which he seemed to think was perfectly in order (despite being the returning officer for an election in which I was a candidate), and that I had been the one to turn the invitation down. Both Sally Powell and Vernon Hince (the Vice-Chair of the Party and a trade union representative from the RMT – the rail-workers' union) spoke about collective trust also requiring collective respect – code for complaining that Millbank didn't play by the rules that they sought to impose on the rest of us.

Throughout the afternoon discussion, Millbank officials scurried in and out of the room engaged in furtive mobile-phone conversations. Sally Morgan, Blair's political assistant, representing him in his absence, had not returned after the lunch-break. Whatever was worrying them, it did not seem to have much to do with the business at hand. There was a discussion about membership of NEC sub-committees. We were not asked which sub-committees we would like to serve on; Millbank simply drew up a list and presented it to us. There was a general trend towards delegating functions away from the NEC itself ("the NEC must be strategic") to sub-committees entirely run by full-timers. Pete muttered, loud enough for everyone to hear, "They'll be abolishing the NEC next." Mark questioned the sub-committee arrangements: "Some of us are worried we'll be put on the flower-arranging sub-committee."

After the NEC away-day, I went to the picket outside the

London Clinic where Pinochet was under arrest. There I was told that Ron Davies MP, the Welsh Secretary, had resigned from the cabinet – that explained the comings and goings at the NEC. Alun Michael soon replaced Davies as Secretary of State and announced that he would be running for Labour Leader in the new Welsh Assembly, against Rhodri Morgan MP (who had lost to Davies only two months earlier). It was no secret that Michael was Blair's candidate. Less than a fornight later, on 9 November 1998, the timetable and arrangements for an electoral college for the selection of the Welsh leader were announced by Party officials. The NEC did not approve the electoral college until a week after the announcement, when the arrangements were already up and running.

There was already widespread discontent in the Welsh Labour Party over the selection of Party candidates for the European Parliament. The Party's candidate lists for the European elections had been drawn up by Millbank officials, who decided the crucial ordering of the list: anyone at the bottom of the regional list stood no chance of winning, and the candidates at the top were virtually guaranteed a seat. Hard-working, well-regarded MEPs, not all of them on the left, were being punished for any independent opinions they might have voiced by being placed so far down the lists that they would have lost out even in a Labour landslide. All the Labour MEPs who had signed an advertisement defending the wording of Clause Four during the Party-wide consultation in 1995 were placed in unwinnable positions. Meanwhile, Millbank's favoured children – some with no experience or local connections at all – were placed above sitting MEPs and guaranteed seats. Michael Cashman was one of these, being placed second on the West Midlands list for the European elections. His apparent links to the region were mocked in Parliament by William Hague: "he once appeared in *The Rocky Horror Show* in Birmingham".

There were stories of slights to decent local MEPs everywhere, and Party members throughout Britain were upset, but in Wales the grievance was acute. An English MEP, Lyndon Harrison, who had not been selected by his local Party members, was ranked third on the Welsh list (out of a total of five seats for the whole region) and ahead of two sitting Welsh MEPs, Joe Wilson and David Morris, who were ranked fourth and fifth, and thus had no chance of re-election. David Morris had faced particular questioning from Labour Party officials over his position as Chair of Welsh CND. Delegates from Wales had protested at the ranking at Conference, but to no avail.

In Scotland, Scottish Labour Party members were seething at various exclusions from the Party's panel of potential candidates for the Scottish Parliament. Several left-wingers had been axed. The best-known was Dennis Canavan, Labour MP for Falkirk West since 1974. Meanwhile, London Labour Party members were beginning to speculate as to whether or not Ken Livingstone would be barred from putting his name forward for selection as the Party's candidate for London mayor. Control-freakery was becoming a word synonymous with New Labour – and a big issue in the Party.

Millbank's response to this growing malaise was to try to shut us all up. The papers for the November NEC meeting, sent out a week in advance, included a "draft code of conduct for NEC members speaking to the media". As with all Millbank documents, the press almost immediately got hold of it; they correctly dubbed it a "gagging clause". The *Guardian* ran "Labour gag on NEC members". Diane Abbott and Diana Jeuda debated its merits on the *Today* programme, where Jeuda conceded that she disagreed with parts of the code. Mark Seddon wrote in the *Independent on Sunday* explaining, "Why I won't be gagged". The code began: "Nothing in this code will be used in an attempt to suppress or silence debate on the NEC or to restrict the right of NEC members to express publicly their views." But NEC members were to "avoid undermining public confidence", to "avoid going head to head with another NEC member and, where possible, with another member of the Labour Party". We were to inform the Millbank press office and seek its advice before discussing NEC business with the media. In other words, while Millbank itself could leak and spin with impunity, we had to clear our every utterance in advance.

As NEC members arrived for their meeting on 17 November, there was a small demonstration by members of Brighton Labour Party. One of their activists, Richard Stanton, had been disciplined by the Labour Party in 1992 for voting against the imposition of the poll tax. His "sentence" was that he was ineligible to stand as a Labour councillor for three years. That time had long expired, and he had put his name forward for selection for the forthcoming 1999 local elections. There seemed no problem, until Millbank had suddenly intervened and declared that he was still ineligible. Brighton Labour Party was protesting, and I handed in a round robin on its behalf. I heard nothing afterward in response to the round robin, and Richard Stanton remained barred from putting his name forward.

Inside Millbank, the NEC met in "the boardroom", a large meeting room with a grand picture window looking out over the Thames. Just as in Blackpool, the top table, consisting of Blair, Etchells, Prescott, McDonagh, Hince and Prosser, was seated with backs to the window and the rest of us facing them. The Thames on a grey November morning was less dramatic than the sunset over the Irish Sea and this time we could see their faces clearly. We were again seated alphabetically, but I swapped with Diana Jeuda so that I could sit next to Cathy Jamieson. This placed me directly opposite Tony Blair. At one point in the meeting I looked up to find him staring fixedly at me. I stared back, and, for a moment, it seemed as if we were trying to outstare each other, like five-year-olds. Everyone – male and female – except Pete wore a suit. Most of the men had taken their jackets off. The women were more tightly buttoned up, and tended to wear bright colours in the now familiar New Labour style. I always stuck to my black work suits.

NEC members used first names in the course of the discussions, but unlike the other members, the Grassroots Alliance representatives refrained from addressing the Prime Minister in this fashion. We were not there because "Tony" was our friend; we were there because we had been elected, and he was there because he was the Leader of the Labour Party. As before, everyone was fairly nervous in our presence. A phalanx of

Millbank staffers, including several press officers, was sitting around the walls. Since the decisions of the NEC can all be predicted, the press officers knew exactly what decisions they would be spinning to the press that day and had no doubt already prepared the press releases. The only mystery to them was what our behaviour would be, and I was uncomfortably aware that they were looking for anything that could be used against us. Blair and Prescott had assistants seated immediately behind them, passing them notes. Sally Morgan always accompanied Blair. There was never any sign of Alastair Campbell. There was a small room off to the side where outside caterers served tea and coffee. A large portrait of Clement Attlee hung on the wall, immediately above Mark and Pete.

Brenda Etchells welcomed everyone to the meeting, saying that she had thought that we were all working together but since the events of the last few days, she was no longer sure. That was a clear reference to the press interest in the gagging clause. We then came to the Prime Minister's report. He started with the recent face-off with Iraq. Three days earlier, the US President Bill Clinton and Tony Blair had ordered airstrikes and bombing raids across Iraq after Saddam Hussein had refused to allow UN arms inspectors access to military sites. Saddam Hussein had climbed down some thirty minutes before cruise missiles were due to be launched. Both Clinton and Blair had said they would not hesitate to attack Iraq without warning in the future. The previous few days had been Saddam's final chance, Blair explained; next time there would be military action. He then launched into what we came to recognise as a familiar pattern. "The only alternative to a Labour government is a Tory government. Party members should all pull together. I can't prevent anyone from speaking to the media, but people have to understand that every time they do so, they are helping the Tories." When he had finished, we were given a chance to ask questions – a precious opportunity, which I worked hard during my two years on the NEC never to waste. Pete, Mark and I all asked about Iraq; Pete noted that military action would involve bombing women and children in Iraq, Mark observed that it would be unlawful to try to assassinate foreign leaders, and I added that the sanctions were not working and were succeeding only in punishing civilians for the crimes of Saddam Hussein. I also said that there was discontent in the Party around perceptions of control-freakery.

In response, Blair said Saddam Hussein had a choice. He would co-operate with UNSCOM – the UN arms inspectors – by allowing inspections of Iraqi weaponry or we would take away his aggressive capacity militarily. Blair denied that sanctions weren't working. He then went on to a complicated rant about control-freakery. He said that Labour Party members (meaning us) were saying that the government was betraying its own people, and that he was entitled to warn the Labour Party of the consequences of such accusations. As for Wales, he couldn't choose the leader there; in Scotland, Canavan had attacked every single decision that the government had taken. "Was that control-freakery or the truth?" he demanded. He also made a reference to an interview for Scottish radio that I had done only that morning – a not very subtle way of letting me know that they were watching and listening and monitoring our every statement. "You guys do as much as you want," Blair concluded. "You will have a ready ear in the media to attack the Labour government. But I will tell the Labour Party where that nonsense leads. It leads to twenty years of Tory government."

Blair left and we moved on to the code of conduct. A revised version had been laid round, although nothing substantive had been amended. The main difference seemed to be that it was now called a "guidance note" rather than a code of conduct. The rest of the morning was taken up with debating it: two and a half hours of a three and a half hour meeting. McDonagh passed round a chronology of the decision making. She referred to a discussion with Mark, and suggested that he had been involved in drawing up the code. He was furious. We were also accused of being disrespectful to Labour Party staff, although in what way was never made clear. It was obvious that we were suspected of leaking the draft code of conduct and there was a surprised silence when I declared, truthfully, that I had not leaked it. Prescott pulled out Mark's *Independent on Sunday* article and started quoting it. Cashman complained that while he was doing a radio interview, Cathy Jamieson had phoned in and that he had therefore been "set up against other NEC members". I pointed out that Cashman had actually been debating with the former Grassroots Alliance candidate Andy Howell on the radio, and that he seemed prepared to debate with a fellow candidate for the NEC, though not a fellow member. He said nothing in response. Sally Powell and Vernon Hince both repeated the remarks they had made at the Congress House meeting about collective trust and collective responsibility, but Hince left before the vote was taken, and Powell said that now the code had been rewritten and was to be called a "guidance note", she would support it. Jeuda said the same thing, despite her previous opposition.

I said that the Grassroots Alliance was elected on a commitment to report to Party members, and that we intended to do that by way of a bulletin. There was much consternation at this and Dianne Hayter (elected to the NEC from the socialist societies) said that if votes were to be recorded, she would vote with the leadership every time. Anne Picking of UNISON wanted the code to include "collective responsibility". Margaret McDonagh summed up, saying that the code would be called a "guidance note" and would be amended to include "collective responsibility". Mark, Pete and Cathy abstained. I voted against, shocked by the sudden inclusive of "collective responsibility" – a concept with no bearing on a diverse, democratic, elected forum like the NEC – and determined not to be silenced. After the meeting had finished, as I was leaving, the Chair warned me to "be careful of the TV outside". So I gave the press a soundbite to the effect that we would not be gagged. The next day the *Guardian* headline was "Davies the lone rebel on NEC rules". The allegation that Mark helped to draft the code was repeated in the article; clearly the account printed by the *Guardian* had effectively been dictated by Millbank. Mark had to write in to correct the falsehood.

Writing in *Tribune* four days later, Paul Anderson named the most prodigious leakers of NEC documents and discussions when he was *Tribune* editor in the early 1990s: David Blunkett, Clare Short, Diana Jeuda, Tom Sawyer and Tony Blair.

I was struck by the difference between Blair and Prescott at the NEC. Blair clearly found the NEC and the Party machinery in general an irritating distraction. His introductory remarks were always fairly peremptory and he appeared to be on autopilot. When he replied, he gushed over the supportive questions and dismissed the difficult ones as quickly as possible. His main aim seemed to be to moan about dissident Labour Party members – and then to leave as soon as he decently could. Over the next two years, I was frequently surprised at how preoccupied Blair was with what he saw as "ungrateful" Labour Party members rocking the boat, and how rarely he would actually engage with any of the political issues raised at the NEC. I also found myself struggling to make sense of some of his responses. He genuinely does speak in short, choppy sentences, often without verbs, and moves relentlessly from one *non sequitur* to another. Unusually for a lawyer, he seems uninterested in arguing his case. He took it for granted that the NEC was there to express appreciation – and seemed to regard it as a personal insult that some of us actually wanted to ask him questions.

Prescott, on the other hand, would usually stay for the duration of the NEC and would engage in arguments. Unlike Blair, he spoke in clear, concise sentences and his point was always understandable. But he never uttered a word that deviated in the slightest from the New Labour message. During Blair's report, he would remain silent, nodding helpfully at certain key messages Blair was trying to deliver. Towards the end of the questions to Blair, Prescott sometimes came in on subjects within his particular responsibility, such as transport. After Blair left the meetings, it was Prescott's job to put the government's or Millbank's line, which he did with total commitment. He came over to me as someone who had spent a lifetime operating in labour movement meetings. He has a more informal, blunt style than Blair and likes to sound down-to-earth, but he knows exactly what he is doing. At an NEC held a year later, he declared, "I bloody hate PR," in what sounded like an off-the-cuff remark. When it found its way into all the newspapers the following day, I realised that it had been pre-arranged and carefully calculated.

Prescott is quick-witted, and utterly cynical. He is also well-briefed by Millbank, and will suddenly take out from his papers a public comment or newspaper article written by a member of the NEC and given to him by the Millbank press office. I have never seen a hint of the much-vaunted division between Prescott and Blair. Every word I heard Prescott utter at the NEC was completely on-message and in unqualified support of the New Labour project. Contrary to his television and parliamentary image, he appears to choose his words with care.

Of course, the apparent New Labour, "Old Labour" distinction between Blair and Prescott is useful for both of them, and for the New Labour project. Whenever New Labour is committed to a policy that appears unpalatable to ordinary Labour Party members, such as cuts to benefits, or privatisation of public services, Prescott plays a useful role. He is able to use his "Old Labour" image to suggest that the policy is really progressive, and deserves the Party's support. He can sell the policies to constituencies that distrust Blair. In reality, however, Blair and Prescott are two sides of the same coin.

On 16 December 1998, the US started to bomb Iraq. On 17 December, Britain joined in. The left and the peace movement organised pickets outside Downing Street. I received numerous letters from Party members and motions passed by Party branches and constituencies condemning the bombing. (Those motions were also sent to Millbank but never received a response.) As a result of the clear groundswell of Party opinion, Mark, Cathy, Pete and I put in a motion to the next NEC (scheduled for the end of January) condemning the bombing. We did not expect to win – indeed we were pretty sure that only the four of us would vote for the motion – but we felt we were making an important and appropriate response to the lobbying we had received from Party members. This was what we had been elected to do.

The outrage at the bombing felt by many grassroots Labour Party members was not shared by the majority of delegates to the Party's National Policy Forum – 175 representatives from constituency parties, trade unions, councillors, MPs and MEPs – most of them hand-picked and loyal to the leadership. The Forum met in

Swansea on 16–17 January, but most delegates seemed much more preoccupied with two other events taking place outside it. The first was the Welsh leadership election, which was rapidly becoming a dirty contest. The National Policy Forum's location in Swansea conveniently allowed senior members of the government – Cook, Prescott, Mowlam – to lobby Welsh Labour Party members and Welsh trade union leaders on Alun Michael's behalf. Tony Blair had visited North Wales the previous day, ostensibly in the course of his routine meetings with Party members. Strangely, there seemed to be a lot of those meetings held in Wales during the Welsh leadership campaign, just as a year later, during the London selection contest, Blair would suddenly develop an interest in meetings with London Party members. Two days before the National Policy Forum met in Swansea, the Welsh AEEU executive had been invited to drinks at Number Ten. On the morning of 16 January, in Swansea, the Welsh AEEU announced that it would be voting for Alun Michael, without balloting its membership. It was widely known that the contest would be extremely close, and Alun Michael's chances of success depended on the trade union and the politicians' sections of the electoral college. Rhodri Morgan was certain to win a majority in the ordinary Party members' section, and had substantial support amongst Welsh Assembly candidates. The AEEU decision was a major boost for Michael – and a slap in the face to most of its members who had been deprived of a chance to express their views.

The second event had to do with Robin Cook, and the prurient interest in his private life. The first instalment of his former wife Margaret Cook's book *A Slight and Delicate Creature* had been published in the *Sunday Times* a week earlier; the second instalment was due on Sunday, 17 January. Cook was the Chair of the National Policy Forum. As he walked into the meeting on the Saturday morning, two women already on the platform, Margaret Wall (MSF NEC member and Vice-Chair of the National Policy Forum) and Margaret Mythen (Millbank officer responsible for the National Policy Forum), burst into applause and rose to their feet, apparently attempting to drum up a supportive standing ovation for the beleaguered Foreign Secretary. Everyone else ignored them, and the two women hurriedly sat down. Cook looked faintly embarrassed. The next day, copies of the *Sunday Times* were everywhere; every single delegate had read the tittle-tattle about his extramarital affair and subsequent remarriage, but not one dared mention it.

The National Policy Forum deliberations occurred in workshops, where drafts of policy documents were discussed in desultory fashion. The documents were also being discussed by Party members in local policy forums and at this stage the National Policy Forum was not supposed to make decisions. The workshops were promoted as brainstorming sessions, where all suggestions would be noted and subsequently incorporated into the policy documents. It was no surprise to find the suggestions that came from Grassroots Alliance supporters were consistently omitted whenever the notes from workshops were read out. We spent a lot of time reminding the note-takers of what we had said in the workshops, to no avail. In a workshop on "Britain in the World", I raised the bombing of Iraq and noted the discontent amongst Party members over this course of action. Cook was sitting at the back of the room, but said nothing. I was told by other National Policy Forum members that the bombing was "popular", both generally and amongst Labour Party members. One smartly dressed Young Labour delegate tried to explain the lack of international support for Britain and the United States by saying that France – which she singled out – was not supportive of bombing "because France had not had the same international historic responsibilities as Britain as it had never had an Empire".

The following weekend I went to a meeting called by the Campaign Against Sanctions and War in Iraq (CASWI). The hall was packed. The main speakers were Ahmed Ben Bella (first President of Algeria), Tony Benn and Dennis Halliday, as well as Sukhdev Reel, someone from the Green Party, and myself. Halliday had been UN assistant secretary-general responsible for the oil-for-food programme to Iraq, but had eventually resigned in protest at the deaths of 6,000 Iraqi children a month as a result of UN sanctions. Sukhdev Reel is the mother of Ricky Reel, a young Asian man murdered in London by racists (but not acknowledged as a racist murder by the police). I informed the meeting that the four Grassroots Alliance NEC members had put down a motion to the Labour NEC condemning the bombing. I warned that nobody should expect the motion to be passed, but given the letters we had received from Party members, and the evident feeling on the bombing issue within the Party, it was important at least to have the debate and state the case.

Four days later, on 26 January, the NEC met at Millbank. As usual, laid round on our seats at the outset of the meeting were additional papers which we had no time to study. This time they included a copy of a letter I had written to George Howarth MP, a junior minister in the Home Office. Barry Horne, an animal rights activist serving a prison sentence for arson, had gone on hunger strike in prison to remind the government that the Labour Party manifesto had promised a royal commission on animal experimentation. No royal commission had been set up. It seemed to me reasonable that the Party should implement its manifesto commitment and I had written to George Howarth saying so. He sent the letter on to Millbank. Brenda Etchells opened the meeting by saying that it was very sad that a member of the NEC had written to George Howarth and copied her letter to Barry Horne, and then added that I had (somehow) "put the lives of Party staff at risk". I was astonished that a polite letter raising a specific question about a particular government policy, addressed to the minister in charge of that policy, could be construed in this way. At no time had I indicated any support for Barry Horne's tactics. Etchells was clearly nervous and wanted to move straight on without giving me the right of reply. I stayed quiet, but after the NEC, I wrote to Etchells complaining about her gross misrepresentation of my actions, and also copied the letter to all the other members of the NEC. I never received a response.

Robin Cook was present at this NEC, although he was not a member. Officially, he was there to introduce the proposed manifesto for the June 1999 European elections – a document concocted with hardly any reference to the Party members. The manifesto explicitly stated the Party's commitment to a single currency, which was a departure in Labour policy. The GMB objected to this and to the failure to mention a referendum. But this division was soon swept under the carpet. We were then assured by Alan Donnelly and Pauline Green MEP (Leader of the Socialist Group in the European Parliament and not a bit player) that the allegations of fraud and mismanagement against some of the European commissioners were unsubstantiated and were nothing but politically motivated attacks on the Socialist commissioners. Within months, the allegations had been upheld, and a number of commissioners were forced to resign.

After the European manifesto had been agreed, the Chair suggested that we take the motion on Iraq from Mark, Pete, Cathy and me, while Cook was still present. I nodded, although I was thinking that the Foreign Secretary would be rather better briefed than me, and I was feeling nervous at taking him on. However, as I opened my mouth to propose the motion, John Allen of the AEEU interrupted with a point of order. He said that since Iraq had been discussed at the previous NEC, the motion was out of order. Mark pointed out that the previous NEC had met in November, and that the bombings had started some weeks later, in December. Clive Soley said that it would be a shame not to hear Robin (Cook) since he was there. So we heard Cook for ten or fifteen minutes justifying the bombings. After he finished speaking, I was all ready to speak to the motion when John Allen again moved that the resolution should not be debated and that the NEC should move to next business. It was obvious that everyone except the four of us was expecting this. Without any further discussion, a vote was taken and "next business" was agreed by nineteen votes to five. The five were the four of us plus Anne Picking from UNISON, who later told the UNISON executive that she voted with us only because she was so opposed to our motion that she wanted to see it voted down. Cook left without having to face any challenge to any of the points he had made in defence of the bombing. A Labour government had engaged in a highly controversial act of war, and the Labour NEC was not to be permitted to discuss or vote upon it.

The NEC then rushed through a short item imposing a £2,000 levy on each constituency Party to pay for the European elections. This proved immensely unpopular, in particular with the smaller constituencies. It felt to them like a poll tax, with no account taken of their means to pay. (£2,000 is a lot of money for many constituency parties.) And given that they were expected to campaign on a manifesto they hadn't drawn up, for candidates they hadn't selected, it really did add insult to injury. Mark explained the objections to the levy, but these were brushed aside.

I was beginning to notice that the NEC consistently ignored the main events taking place in the real world, not least the various crises affecting the Labour government. When it did refer to them, it was only to dismiss any difficulties as due to trouble-makers in the media. Peter Mandelson had been forced to resign from the cabinet shortly before Christmas after the revelations about his loan from Geoffrey Robinson. This was a major blow for Blair, who had come to depend on Mandelson, and a pro-found embarrassment to the Party, which prided itself on rising above "Tory sleaze". But the only reference to these events at the NEC was Blair's bland comment that "it was a difficult Christmas". He then retreated to his favourite theme of blaming the media ("the media push an agenda around scandal, gossip and trivia") or Labour Party members ("the Labour Party is in a constant state of dialogue with its own leadership"). There was a proposal to commission a feasibility study on whether the work of the mem-bership department should be put out to private tender, which we voted against. The GMB, which represents Labour Party staff whose jobs would be lost if the membership department was privatised, abstained. As we were voting, Pete commented that feasibility studies always recommended what they were told to recommend. (The truth of this observation was to be borne out four months later, when the feasibility study reported to the NEC.) We then spent most of the rest of the meeting discussing the "Bermuda triangle" again.

3

The New Paymasters

In Millbank documents, the devil is in the detail and the detail is usually at the back. The National Executive Committee Annual Report, presented to Conference each year, consists largely of puff pieces by the General Secretary, exhortations to "campaign", and glossy photographs of MPs, Millbank staff and NEC members. At the very back are the financial accounts for the preceding year.

The 1998 Annual Report contained a section headed: "Disclosure of financial support in 1997" – a list of donors who had given donations or sponsorship in excess of £5,000. No figures were given: it was impossible to tell whether a particular donor had given £5,001, £50,000 or £1,000,000. From the accounts, one would not know that Bernie Ecclestone's donation was as much as £1,000,000 or that the accompanying footnote "this donation was made and repaid during the financial year" referred to the first sleaze scandal to hit New Labour.

The list headed "Sponsorship" made interesting reading. Only three individuals were named; one of them was Geoffrey Robinson. Four trade unions and the Co-Operative Wholesale Society were listed. The rest of the names – thirty in all – were companies, most of them multinationals.

According to guidelines which I found in an internal Party document: "the Labour Party will not accept donations from companies the activities of which are inconsistent with the principles of the Labour Party", nor will it accept foreign-sourced donations. Yet, in 1997, the Party accepted payments, in excess of £5,000 each, from, among many others, Raytheon Systems Ltd, Enron Europe Ltd, British American Financial Services, and

Novartis Pharmaceuticals UK Ltd. All of these companies are either based in the USA, or are subsidiaries of companies based in the USA.

Raytheon Systems Ltd is one of the world's three largest arms manufacturers. It makes Tomahawk, Patriot, Sidewinder and Stinger missiles. It supplies arms to Saudi Arabia, Malaysia, Singapore, Brunei, Indonesia and Thailand, among others. It is based in the USA and has been found to be in breach of US labour law on a number of occasions. It has declined an invitation from Human Rights Watch to cease production of land mines. In 1999, it was awarded an £800 million contract by the Ministry of Defence.

Enron Europe Ltd is a subsidiary of the US power company Enron. The parent company is the largest private power corporation in the Indian subcontinent. It has been the subject of a report by Amnesty International condemning its human rights abuses. Amnesty reported that in 1997 local police arrived at a village in Dhobal, near Bombay. Close to the village was the subcontinent's largest power plant, built and operated by Enron. The villagers had protested at destruction of their livelihood – the fisheries and coconut and mango trees that were being polluted by effluent from the power plant. The police arrived when the men of the village were out fishing. They turned their batons on women and children, beating them and imprisoning hundreds of women. Amnesty reported that Enron security staff were involved and said that the police had been paid for by the company for that operation. In 1999, Enron was awarded the Wessex Water franchise in a £1.5 billion deal. The franchise gave Enron a monopoly over water supply to the South-West of England, yet the Labour government refused to refer the bid to the Monopolies Commission. Its contribution to Labour Party funds is said to be £30,000 since 1997, and the decision not to refer the bid was announced three weeks after Enron gave £15,000 to Party funds at a gala fundraising dinner in October 1998. In the 2001 New Year's honours list, Enron Europe's chairman was awarded a CBE by Tony Blair. Meanwhile, in India, Enron is under siege from public protests about the cynical way it is bankrupting the state-run electricity supplier in Maharashtra. In the USA, Enron has been the largest single contributor to George W. Bush's campaign fund.

British American Financial Services Ltd used to be controlled by British American Tobacco. Its most famous public face is Allied Dunbar, one of the firms exposed in the pensions mis-selling scandal. Novartis Pharmaceuticals UK Ltd is part of the Novartis conglomerate, one of the world's giants in the development of genetically modified foods. It sponsors at least one Labour MP.

At the same October 1998 Conference that received (but did not discuss) the 1997 list of donors, the supermarket chain Somerfield sponsored the neck tags on which delegates' credentials were hung. Many Conference delegates were uncomfortable at being required to advertise a privately owned supermarket chain. The GMB produced its own neck tags, with the GMB logo, and did a roaring trade as delegates swapped their blue-and-white Somerfield tags for red GMB ones.

Supermarkets have been among New Labour's most consistent financial supporters: Safeway, Sainsbury and Tesco in 1997, Somerfield and Tesco in 1998 (Sainsbury having decided that sponsorship of political parties infringed its own rules against political donations), and Tesco again in 1999 (having both sponsored the Party for the mysterious "£5,000 or more" and bought tickets for gala dinners worth at least £5,000).

Also at the October 1998 Conference, speakers at fringe meetings recounted in some detail how UNICEF, an exhibitor at Conference, had been asked by Labour Party staff to remove posters campaigning against the use of bottled baby milk in the Third World. It seemed that they might be objectionable to another exhibitor at the conference, Nestlé, purveyor of baby milk powder and the target of a long-running international campaign against the promotion of baby milk powder in the Third World. Four months later, in response to published reports of this incident, Margaret Prosser, Treasurer of the Party, stated in a letter to *Tribune* that the removal of the posters had nothing to do with Nestlé's presence; all that had happened was that

UNICEF was asked to remove posters that had been placed outside its own stall.

The love affair between New Labour and big business is increasingly the subject of comment by the media and Party members alike. Conference 1998 looked more like a big-money football club – corporate logos were ubiquitous – than a labour movement gathering. Cabinet ministers were more likely to attend fundraising dinners or corporate sponsored receptions than they were to address fringe meetings. The press reported on lobbyist firms booking tables at the Party's gala dinner at £200 per head or £2,000 for a table.

All this deeply troubled me. As a member of the Party's NEC, I felt I had a responsibility to scrutinise our accounts, and to be able to assure myself that the Party was above reproach. There could be no doubt that a number of the donations and sponsorships were profoundly compromising, and deeply offensive to a large number of the Party's own members. Donations and sponsorship also raised the broader public interest issue of the links between government and big business, an issue I believed the Labour NEC – formally the governing body of the governing Party – had an obligation to address.

At that January 1999 NEC meeting, Cathy Jamieson and I had proposed a motion calling for a general review of Labour Party policy on donations, sponsorship, advertising and exhibiting at Party conferences and similar activities. Most importantly, our motion called for the establishment of criteria for the acceptance of sponsorships – criteria that reflected Labour's values and the need for the Party (and the government) to be and to be seen to be independent of special interests. We had in mind the establishment of ethical criteria for the acceptance of payments, similar to guidelines for ethical investment funds that most investment companies now offer. I could not believe that taking money from arms traders, for example, would be acceptable to the majority of Party members. Cathy and I were also concerned that government decision making should not be seen to be influenced by conflicts of interest – actual or apparent.

The public makes the reasonable assumption that companies

give money to political parties in the expectation of receiving something in return. The "something" need not be tangible – the opportunity to meet a cabinet minister at a social event, or to be informed of government thinking in advance. Lobbyists make a good living selling access to information within the "loop". Sometimes, though, the benefits seem all too tangible. Many of the major players in privatised utilities feature in the Party's lists of donors or sponsors: BT, Scottish Power, British Gas, Northumbria Water, Railtrack, Connex Rail, SEEBoard, Severn Trent plc. They each have interests in government decisions regulating their industry, and in re-bidding for their franchises. The major supermarkets, Sainsbury, Tesco, Safeway and Somerfield, all have direct interests in government decisions on food safety and regulations, on the minimum wage, and in planning decisions on out-of-town shopping centres. Some companies are directly bidding for government contracts: Raytheon, the utility companies, British Aerospace. Mobile phone companies, such as One 2 One, have interests in government decisions on regulation, as does Rupert Murdoch's BSkyB. Drug companies, such as Pfizer Ltd or Novartis Ltd, have interests in decisions on GM foods, and in NHS drug purchasing. Yet the Labour Party has accepted payments of one kind or another from all of them since entering government in 1997.

The concern broadly felt across the Labour Party about all of this was simply not shared by the majority of NEC members or the Millbank staff. As required by the NEC rules, Cathy and I had submitted our motion fourteen days in advance of the meeting. I then received a call from David Pitt-Watson urging me to withdraw the motion. He told me that a "review" was already in progress. I asked what the review's timetable would be, to get some idea of when this (increasingly urgent) matter could be discussed at the NEC, but Pitt-Watson declined to answer the question. Having consulted with Cathy, I rang back and told him that under the circumstances we could not agree to withdraw the motion. He told me that he was very disappointed and that clearly we were not "serious" about Party finances. This was Pitt-Watson's technique, suggesting that we could either take the public ("confrontational") route and thereby achieve nothing, or behave ourselves, submit to Millbank's tutelage, and thereby come to have some unspecified influence at some unspecified time. After Pitt-Watson failed with me, he tried the same argument with Cathy, with equal lack of success. He finally gave up on this after *Tribune* published an article by me explaining the concerns that had led us to propose our motion.

According to the minutes of the Finance Sub-committee submitted to the January NEC, the Finance Sub-committee had already taken a decision to remit our motion to themselves (though it had not been submitted to them, but to our colleagues on the NEC as a whole). These minutes were formally moved and seconded at the NEC. Margaret Prosser said that it was very sad that we had not agreed to remit the motion, and that my writing in *Tribune* was even more sad. We were told, again, that a review was already in progress. I was invited to attend this review. I accepted the invitation and was just about to speak to the motion when we were told, suddenly, that the minutes of the Finance Sub-committee having been proposed and seconded meant that they had been accepted and that therefore the decision to remit our motion to themselves had been endorsed. Brenda Etchells in the chair ruled our motion out of order, and then moved to other business – with no further discussion or vote of any kind. At the end of the meeting, I watched Pitt-Watson deep in conversation with Mark and Pete. He was trying on the same message that had failed with Cathy and me, and would also fail with them.

On 6 February, the *Daily Mail* ran precisely the story that Cathy and I had been warning about. Under the headline "Labour's links to gene foods: chemical giant spent thousands of pounds on Party meeting", it reported that Novartis had paid for a seminar for newly elected Labour MPs in 1997 and that its officials were visiting the agriculture ministry on an almost daily basis. The *Daily Mail*, happy to seize on any excuse to bash the Labour Party, speculated that the government's fudging on GM foods was related to the Party's links with Novartis.

And what of our motion calling for a review and the establishment of criteria for the acceptance of sponsorship? After that

January NEC, I wrote to David Pitt-Watson asking for the timetable of the review. He replied that at the March meeting of the Finance Sub-committee, the committee would consider a future framework for sponsorship, donations and the Party's other financial activities. The Finance Sub-committee met on 1 March 1999 and, at that meeting, agreed to set up a review of the Party's financial relations. Eight days later, the Finance Sub-committee held an "away-day" to discuss the future financial strategy of the Party. Notes of the away-day were circulated to the NEC. The first item discussed was "high-value fund-raising" and the notes read: "The balance of funding of the Party will involve more high-value funding. It was agreed that we need to stop being apologetic about this." A letter was to be written to Lord Levy, proposing plans for fundraising in the year 2000.

One of these high-value fundraising activities took place on 16 April 1999, when Blair hosted a £500-a-head dinner at the Hilton Hotel in London. The press later revealed that at this dinner, over £5.47 million worth of donations and pledges were made by thirty-one businessmen. Amongst them was Isaac Kaye, who gave £100,000. Isaac Kaye is chairman of Norton Healthcare, one of Britain's biggest "generic drugs" manufacturers, and deputy chief executive of its US parent company, Ivax Corporation, based in Miami. Norton Healthcare does not recognise trade unions. The company was censured in 1996 for offering inappropriate inducements to pharmacists to increase their orders for Norton products. The prices charged for their drugs have been cited as amongst the worst instances of overcharging to the NHS. Kaye has been a regular donor to New Labour since at least 1997. He also gave £10,000 to Frank Dobson's campaign to be selected as Labour candidate for London mayor. Another pledge of £100,000 came from Gulam K. Noon, millionaire chairman of Noon Products and another non-recogniser of trade unions.

In May 1999, I drafted a five-page submission to the Party's "review" of its financial relations (see Appendix 2). I argued the case for criteria for the receipt of sponsorship to include ethical considerations and avoidance of any apparent conflicts of interest. I had another telephone conversation with Pitt-Watson, in which he told me that there was a lot more sympathy for my position than I might expect, but that sympathy would evaporate if I started to use the press to raise the issues. So I sent in my submission, in confidence, as requested. And I heard nothing. Finally, five months later, in October 1999, at Party Conference, figuring that the agreement with Pitt-Watson had long since expired, I wrote an article for the *Morning Star* setting out my concerns and proposals, and I distributed copies of my submission to Conference delegates.

The list of donors for 1998, presented to Conference in October 1999 – not to mention the atmosphere at the Conference itself – confirmed that Millbank and Blair had no intention of changing course on big business links. In 1998, Raytheon's lobbyists bought "tickets for dinners", and the Labour Party also received "over £5,000" from British Aerospace, Raytheon's competitor. In British Aerospace's eyes, Robin Cook's announcement in June 1997 that foreign policy would be conducted with an "ethical dimension" must have appeared ominous. At the time, they were contracted to the Indonesian government to supply sixteen Hawk fighters, at a cost of £350 million. No Hawk fighters had yet been delivered, and there were widespread allegations that Hawks had been used over East Timor. Cook was well aware that the Indonesian government used Hawk aircraft to intimidate the East Timorese – he had attacked the Tories in the Commons on that very point when Labour was in opposition. Cancelling the contract would have been entirely in accord with the new ethical policy. But the contract was not cancelled. All sixteen Hawks were delivered to the Indonesian government. In August and September 1999, the world watched appalled as the East Timorese were slaughtered for daring to vote for independence. Hawk aircraft were reported to be in action once again over Dili, the capital of East Timor. The sale of arms to Indonesia was not cancelled by the Labour government until September 1999, by which time the Indonesian military had already wreaked havoc in East Timor. In January 2000, the government quietly resumed the sale of arms to Indonesia. Five senior British Aerospace executives received honours in January 2001.

The 1998 accounts also displayed a new heading, to the best of my knowledge not one commonly used in accountancy practice. Under the heading "Tickets for dinners", a number of lobbyist firms are listed. They include Lawson Lucas & Mendelsohn Ltd (exposed in the Derek Draper affair as selling "cash for access"), GJW (whose clients include Balfour Beatty, Lockheed Martin, Nestlé and Raytheon, and who used to employ Draper) and the ubiquitous Isaac Kaye. The "tickets for dinners" ruse is designed to permit lobbyists to book their clients places at fundraising dinners without using clients' own names – thus disguising the real nature of the association. The clients can attend safe in the knowledge that their presence – and links with the government – are hidden from public scrutiny.

In 1998, for the first time in the Party's history, money contributed by trade unions was matched by money raised from "high value donors". The Party was working deliberately to shift the revenue balance away from trade union money (and influence) towards big business money (and influence). And that strategy was naked at the 1999 Conference. The *Daily Telegraph* reported that, out of 20,000 people attending Conference, only 1,500 were Party or trade union delegates. 18,500 were lobbyists, business representatives or journalists. Supermarket logos may have been removed from around delegates' necks, but there were more exhibitors than ever before. The day of the Prime Minister's speech was a fundraising extravaganza. For £700, a corporate executive could purchase breakfast with government ministers, a ringside seat to watch the Prime Minister deliver his speech to Conference and attendance at an evening cocktail party to meet cabinet ministers. Donors who had given more than £25,000 to the Party were treated to a free private lunch with cabinet ministers before Blair's speech, and tea with the Prime Minister immediately after he had delivered his speech. The fundraising gala dinner was marketed at £350 a head, was attended by cabinet ministers, and was sponsored by Manchester Airport plc. The conference was said to have raised over £1.5 million for Party finances.

When my *Morning Star* article was published during that 1999

conference, David Pitt-Watson called it "disgraceful". Attending
Conference was his last act as the Party's finance director. He
resigned shortly after, and sent all of us on the NEC a letter
promoting his new private consultancy. His successor, Howard
Attridge, lasted only three months.

Finally, in November 1999, six months after I had submitted
my proposals, I was invited to attend a meeting of the review. It
was chaired by Keith Ewing, professor of law at King's College
London, and met in Millbank. Elsewhere in the building on that
day, Ken Livingstone was being interviewed by the Party's London
Selection Board, who would decide whether or not to allow him
on to the shortlist for London mayor. The cameras gathered
outside Millbank, and inside the atmosphere was buzzing, though
not at the review. At the meeting were Keith Ewing, Margaret
Prosser (present as Party Treasurer), Vernon Hince and Sally
Powell (local government representative on the NEC), together
with two officers, Jonathan Upton and Amanda Delew (head of
high-value fundraising). Ewing introduced the meeting by saying
that the review had been set up in March 1999 – confirming my
suspicion that, contrary to what we were told at the January NEC,
there had been no review or even any thought of a review prior
to our motion.

In any case, I was glad that finally these concerns might be
addressed and that my paper would get discussed at some level.
At the meeting, Margaret Prosser seemed to have given herself
the task of disagreeing, as a matter of principle, with everything I
said. We talked through some of the ideas in my submission, on
conflicts of interest and ethical standards. Ewing suggested that a
Labour government putting through employment law reform
might be considered as acting according to the interests of trade
unions, and that would be a conflict of interest. I suggested that
the electorate tended to expect that a Labour government would
be more favourable to the trade unions than the Tories, that that
was a question of ideology and policy, and that the trade unions
were actually part of the Party, which could not be said about the
private sector. As I was making a secondary point that employment law reform benefits individual trade union members rather

than trade unions as institutions, Prosser interjected at length about employment law reform resulting in an increase in trade union membership. Vernon Hince said very little, but nodded away, so he appeared to be in full agreement with whoever was speaking. Sally Powell engaged with the issues and said that she had particularly strong feelings against companies which use child labour.

We had a long discussion about the ethics of the arms trade, Prosser arguing that Labour Party members were perfectly comfortable with taking money from this source. It was an integral part of the economy like any other, she said, and if it provided jobs why shouldn't we take money from it? I suggested a consultation of Labour Party members. By the end of the meeting, no conclusions had been reached and no plans had been indicated for further consultation. Two weeks after the meeting, on 30 November 1999, *The Times* reported that senior officials in the Party were sympathetic to my views on funding and quoted Keith Ewing as saying that he would "consider very seriously" my submission. Since then, I have heard absolutely nothing on any of these matters from any member of the "review".

The deliberations of the "review" were never reported to the NEC or, as far as I could see, to the Party's Finance Sub-committee. In fact, after that meeting in November, it was never heard of again. I can only conclude that the whole process was a sham, entered into in an attempt to stifle the issues I was raising, and that, contrary to the assurances of Pitt-Watson and Ewing, Party officials never had the slightest intention of reviewing their policy of fundraising from big business.

In April 2000, the Party held a fundraising dinner at the Grosvenor House Hotel. Tickets for this event were £500 a head (or, the invitation advertised, tables of ten could be purchased at £5,000 – so no bulk discounts under New Labour). Neil Kinnock personally invited me – at least in writing – along with other members of the NEC, to attend (free) as the Party's guest that evening. I was delighted to turn the invitation down.

At Conference 2000, the accounts for 1999 were published. Again, money from big business (described as "high value donations" and "commercial activities") amounted to some 30 per cent of the Party's income – the same proportion as given by the trade unions. As if the clusters of privatised utilities (British Gas, SEEBoard, Severn Trent plc), rail operators (Connex), air operators (British Midland and Manchester Airport) and mobile phone companies (One 2 One) were not sufficiently "inconsistent with the principles of the Labour Party" as per the guidelines that then existed, the Party now also accepted money from the US fast-food chain McDonald's. Indeed, McDonald's has become an enthusiastic sponsor of the government's Education Action Zones, teaching primary school children to sing "Old McDonald Had a Store" and to recognise images of its French fries and milk shakes in apparently educational materials. McDonald's regard their access to children through their sponsorship of schools as an excellent marketing opportunity. No doubt their munificence towards New Labour (in whatever amount in excess of £5,000) is commercially justified as helping to ensure that their sponsorship of Education Action Zones can continue, in spite of growing protests.

Conference 2000 did nothing to buck the fundraising trend. Again, lobbyists and representatives from big business outnumbered constituency and trade union delegates by around ten to one. Big business paid for exhibition stalls and adverts in the glossy conference papers, and sponsored various fringe meetings. It felt more like a trade fair than a conference. The adverts for some of the fringe meetings read like inadvertent self-parodies: "Tackling Debt and Financial Exclusion: Whose Responsibility?" – sponsored by Barclays, "Tackling Fuel Poverty and Improving Consumer Confidence" – sponsored by Powergen, "Kids Club Network" – sponsored by Nestlé. The speakers at these meetings routinely include government ministers as well as corporate publicists. It doesn't really matter what is said or how poorly attended the meeting is – a bond is being forged.

In the pack of official conference documents, Nestlé offered delegates "a challenge – how healthy is the food you eat and how does it compare to current recommendations?" and a free consultation with a nutritionist. During that consultation, Nestlé would take the opportunity to inform the delegate "how we are helping to meet the daily nutritional needs of all the family". Merck Sharp & Dome (a leading pharmaceutical manufacturer) was offering a free blood pressure and cholesterol check. McDonald's, in a half-page advert in the conference brochure, announced, "McDonald's is committed to putting something back into the local communities it serves."

Unlike the previous two years, however, the media paid scant attention to the corporate presence at Conference. New Labour's eagerness to snuggle up to big business had become such a familiar spectacle that neither the media nor the delegates could any longer blink an eye at it.

The public and the media do, however, blink when it comes to donations on the scale of £2 million each from multi-millionaires. The Party's recent fundraising scandals – Robert Bourne's donation of £100,000 to Party funds apparently unconnected with the proposed sale of the Dome to his company; £2 million donations each from Lords Hamlyn and Sainsbury, and from Christopher Ondaatje – provoked precisely the media criticism that I had been warning about. The Party's initial refusal to come clean suggested that it knew only too well that the public wonders what these multi-millionaires receive in return. The position of Lord Sainsbury, who has now given the Party a total of £6 million, is particularly questionable. He is an unelected member of the government, having been appointed to the House of Lords by Blair to enable him to join the government. Lord Sainsbury has substantial interests in research into GM foods and, of course, as owner of the Sainsbury chain, in food safety and prices. As a member of the government, all his personal finances have been placed in a "blind trust" and he claims to leave the room whenever GM foods or other matters in which he has an interest are discussed. But, as Minister for Science at the Department of Trade and Industry, the politician said to be Britain's richest man oversees competition policy.

At no time during my two years on the NEC did any of its members outside the left show the slightest interest in any of the financial embarrassments to hit New Labour. There were no attempts to learn lessons from the Bernie Ecclestone affair. Nobody seemed interested in considering how to prevent conflicts of interest. Indeed, there was little or no financial scrutiny by the NEC. An annual budget was presented only once during the two years, in January 2000. The budget consisted of two sides of paper, with some proposals for additional expenditure, but with no actual figures or balance sheets attached. It was impossible to tell from the paper how much the Party's annual income and expenditure was, or how the expenditure was allocated. I have sat on a local authority finance committee, and on countless management committees of voluntary organisations. All of those bodies scrutinised their finances and considered their budgets in far more detail than the NEC did. Accounts were never presented to the NEC – although each Annual Report to Conference refers to the NEC drawing up financial statements. In general, members of the NEC seemed to display a cavalier attitude to the Party's finances, and an even more cavalier attitude to the source of some of the donations.

The questions about Lord Sainsbury's position, about the Ecclestone affair, and about the Robert Bourne donation all show New Labour's extraordinary insensitivity to the need to avoid apparent conflicts of interest. Mandelson's lack of judgement in trying to progress a passport application for the Hinduja brothers, when they were also major donors to the Dome, is another example. The individual donations raise serious questions about conflicts of interest regarding particular individuals and government decisions. But, over and above any individual scandals, New Labour's willingness to take money from big business must raise questions about government policy. New Labour's agenda of privatisation is deeply attractive to big business, which stands to benefit directly. The increasing dependence of the Party on donations from big business, rather than contributions from trade unions and local parties, means that big business wields an influence over policy denied to Party members. And the policies of privatisation and tax breaks for the rich, which big business requires from New Labour, are policies unacceptable to most ordinary Party members.

From February 2001, all political parties are required to disclose names and actual amounts of all donations or sponsorship monies in excess of £5,000. New Labour's desperation to keep its large donations secret for as long as possible has lost it the opportunity to seize the moral high ground from the Tories, and given it a reputation for "sleaze" rapidly overtaking even the Tories.

4

New Labour in Deep Denial

In February 1999, I went to the Guildhall in Swansea to speak at a meeting called by the Swansea Labour Left. It was held on 20 February, the night before the announcement of the result of the contest for Labour Leader in the Welsh Assembly. Chairing the meeting was David Morris MEP, who had been put fifth on the Welsh list for the European Parliament elections (see page 32), and had then withdrawn in protest. The place was buzzing. Rhodri Morgan was the popular choice as Leader for Welsh Party members – and the man whom Blair appeared determined to keep out. The audience of Labour activists were all Morgan supporters and included the two Welsh Assembly candidates for Swansea, Val Fell and Andrew Davies (one of Morgan's campaign managers). The result was still very much up in the air and although the trade union votes meant that the Millbank-backed candidate Alun Michael probably had the edge, the Morgan camp were cheerful and optimistic. They were going to Cardiff the next day for the announcement.

During the course of the Welsh leadership contest Millbank had displayed the same flagrant disregard for democratic norms and official neutrality as it had in the National Executive Committee contest six months earlier. It was apparent that the Alun Michael camp had privileged knowledge of the date on which ballot papers were to be sent out to Welsh Party members, and Millbank had lobbied the Welsh press to carry puff pieces for Michael at the appropriate moment. At that same time, identical letters were sent out by MPs to their Party members, urging support for Michael. Peter Hain, in an attempt both to discredit

UNISON's ballot result for Morgan and to smear Morgan at the same time, claimed that UNISON members who voted for Morgan were a bunch of "Trotskyists". And, according to Paul Flynn MP, the Michael campaign appeared to have been informed of the result prior to the actual announcement. These tactics were to be used again by Millbank less than a year later in the selection of a candidate for London mayor, as was the oft-repeated claim that the electoral college used in Wales and London was the same as that used to elect Tony Blair and John Prescott in 1994. In fact, in the election for Leader of the Party in 1994, the rules prohibited trade unions from participating in the electoral college if they had not balloted their members. Had all trade unions been required to ballot their members in Wales and in London, Morgan would have won in 1999 and Livingstone in 2000.

The company conducting the Party's internal ballot process, Unity Security Balloting Ltd, had also conducted the NEC elections. It is a company funded and controlled by trade unions. In the Welsh leadership campaign of 1999, as in the NEC contest of 1998, and the London mayoral selection in 2000, advance leaks of the ballot results turned out to be amazingly accurate. In any case, Alun Michael was officially declared the winner of the Welsh leadership election on 21 February 1999. Paul Flynn MP described the feeling that night: "the Labour Party in Wales was ashamed of itself. We were preparing our own catastrophe." The leadership campaign had demoralised Welsh Labour Party members, who saw their democratic choice for Leader pushed aside as a result of manipulation from Millbank. Ordinary members were not motivated to fight the Assembly elections and the leadership contest had given Labour's opponents plenty of ammunition.

The NEC met on 23 March – six weeks before the Welsh, Scottish and local elections (due to be held on 6 May). The meeting completely ignored the shattering and widely publicised events in the Welsh Labour Party, and spent very little time discussing the forthcoming elections. It preferred instead to spend most of its time discussing internal "codes of conduct" to regulate the forthcoming NEC elections. The Grassroots Alliance had made a point of campaigning for a regulatory code. After the previous year's elections, and after the attacks launched by Tom Sawyer, we wanted to ensure that Party staff were neutral, and we also wanted to see a spending limit so that all candidates could campaign on a level playing field. The code that we were presented with did little to allay either concern.

The proposed code of conduct had been sent out in advance to NEC members – and inevitably to selected members of the press. The *Today* programme rang me on the morning of the meeting asking for a comment. I said I would only give them one after the meeting. The NEC proceedings began with the Chair's usual little homily – a number of members were said to be "very unhappy" with the reports of the NEC meetings that Mark was publishing in *Tribune*. She moved on hurriedly, without giving Mark the opportunity to reply. Blair then repeated his familiar message – "people always want everything the day before yesterday" – and recited the familiar litany of his government's achievements. There was no reference to the divisions in the Welsh Party or any concern about the results of the coming elections. Indeed, he described the Party as being "in better stead than for a long period".

Blair came under heavy fire, unexpectedly, from Vernon Hince of the RMT, who was very angry about Millbank's recent performance. He said "sometimes we don't send the right signals". He was incensed that John Reid, then Minister for Transport, had condemned the London underground workers for conducting a legal strike and had refused to meet them, but had been happy to meet with the road haulage blockade. "Sometimes the signals aren't helping," Hince repeated. When Blair replied, he said that John Reid had condemned both the road hauliers and the tube strikers. As far as the tube workers were concerned, Blair said that all John Reid had said was "the strike was unjustified and would damage their own cause". Hince muttered loudly: "I never thought I'd hear a Labour prime minister say that." Later Prescott weighed in, saying that the tube workers were attacking the Labour Party in opposing public–private partnership for the tube, and dismissing Hince's complaint with the observation, "There's an election going on in the RMT." Hince was indeed at that

moment campaigning to retain his position as RMT Deputy
General Secretary, and Prescott rarely passes up a chance to
obfuscate the issue by commenting on the critic's motivation.

Although you wouldn't have known it from the tenor and
priorities of that NEC meeting, the British Labour government
was at that very moment on the brink of war with Yugoslavia. In
his opening remarks, Blair outlined his position in the Kosova
crisis. He said that "we" would have to act for three reasons: there
was a humanitarian disaster, the violence might spill out to the
whole of the region, and the credibility of NATO was at stake. I
said that bombing would not be the solution to the Serbian
atrocities, that it was punishing innocent civilians for the crimes
of Milosevic, and that it was likely to reinforce his support, just as
bombing had reinforced Saddam Hussein's support. Military
action through NATO, not the United Nations, could not be
justified, and set a dangerous precedent. The Prime Minister
replied that a UN resolution would be blocked by Russia or
China, and insisted that thanks to bombings "Saddam Hussein is
back in his box".

We then moved on to the report from the European Parliament, which was in stark contrast to the anodyne assurances we
had received only two months earlier. In the meantime, the
European Commission had resigned *en masse* after an inquiry into
allegations of fraud had reported that the Commission was
responsible for a culture of cronyism, mismanagement and fraud.
Alan Donnelly repeated his claim that the Tories and Liberals
were targeting Socialist commissioners, but then conceded that
the inquiry's report was devastating and that the only way to
ensure that Jacques Santer and Edith Cresson resigned was for
the whole Commission to resign.

After Blair left, the bulk of the meeting was spent on the
proposed code of conduct for NEC ballots. Under this code,
candidates would be prohibited from questioning the integrity of
the conduct of the ballot. If candidates had complaints, they were
to give them in confidence to "the independent scrutineer" –
another name for Unity Security Balloting Ltd, the organisation
conducting the ballot. The decision of USB was to be final,

although USB would have the right to refer complaints to the General Secretary and the NEC. Candidates would not have the same right. So USB would be investigating itself, and candidates would have no recourse to an independent investigation. There were to be no spending limits. Party membership lists would not be given to any candidates, although everyone knew that the effect of that prohibition would be that some favoured candidates would have access to them and others would not. (The Grassroots Alliance was in favour of all candidates being given membership lists.) Candidates would be prohibited from making attacks on each other in public or in the media – a prohibition that had theoretically applied in 1998, when Grassroots Alliance candidates were repeatedly attacked in public by the General Secretary, the former leader of the Party, and a variety of Millbank apparatchiks. If candidates complained in public about the ballot, they could be subject to disciplinary procedures and could even be excluded from the ballot and from any future ballots. Thus any complaints about the process would be known only to the USB and not to Labour Party members. The timing of the ballot was to be brought forward so that it would take place in May and June 1999– during a period in which the Party would be fighting a series of local and regional elections and no Party meetings would be taking place. The timing of the 1999 ballot would set a precedent for subsequent years; it was obvious that Millbank had given up any hope of retaking all six constituency places, and just wanted to bury the NEC elections in obscurity. It preferred to announce the results halfway through June by means of a muted press release, rather than have to read them out in Conference, before delegates and the media.

During the debate on the code, it became clear that members of the NEC had been specifically lined up to attack the Grassroots Alliance. Whatever we said was condemned; I had the impression that I could move a resolution to the effect that "the earth is round" and most members of the NEC would vote against it. When the four of us voiced concerns about the code, in particular the procedure to restrict complaints, we were accused of bringing USB, and therefore the whole of the Labour Party, into disrepute by our words. Readers should be aware that "bringing the Labour Party into disrepute" is not an accusation to be made idly in Labour Party circles. "A sustained course of conduct which in the opinion of the National Constitutional Committee is prejudicial, or any act which in the opinion of the NCC is grossly detrimental to the Party" is generally referred to as "bringing the Party into disrepute" and usually results in expulsion. Since it is impossible to define satisfactorily – indeed the rule itself leaves the definition up to the NCC – this clause has been used to expel a number of socialists from the Party and to silence a great many others. Accusing us of bringing the Party into disrepute by complaining about USB's conduct of the balloting process was therefore a most serious threat. Sarah Ward said that "we all know the reasons why" candidates questioned the independence of the process. This was not an admission that the process was unsatisfactory in any way, but an assertion of the Millbank paranoid assumption that the Grassroots Alliance thought there was political capital to be made out of attacking the ballot process. Michael Cashman claimed that attacks on USB were "about undermining the Labour Party and the leadership". I had visions of the entire structure of government collapsing if a candidate uttered even a mild complaint about an internal Party balloting process. Cashman's words seemed something of an overstatement. Mike Griffiths (trade union representative from the GPMU) backed away a little from the concept that the government might fall, but claimed that we were engaged in a tactic "to discredit the Labour Party by constant innuendo".

Pete was the first of the four of us to move an amendment. He called for NEC candidates to be required to publish their accounts and to list sources of all donations above £5,000 (in line with the Party's own practice). The Chair told him that he could not move this amendment, because he had been present at the Organisation Sub-committee (where the code had been discussed) and had made the same point there and therefore could not be given two bites at the cherry. There was nothing in the rule book to this effect, but that did not deter the Chair. In discussion, Pete's amendment was pooh-poohed by other NEC members who claimed, falsely, that he was trying to impose publication of accounts retrospectively on the 1998 election. They thus conveniently avoided addressing the real issue: whether there should be publication of accounts in the future. I moved deletion of the clause forbidding public comment on the process. (For the record, I noted also that Rhodri Morgan had only complained after the ballot had closed and that my complaint in 1998 had been sent in a private letter to the General Secretary, and it was the General Secretary who had press-released it.) Mark, who had publicly criticised USB after the Welsh result, proposed that the balloting process in future should be put out to tender and should not always be conducted by the USB. He also proposed a genuinely independent scrutineer, separate from both USB and the Party. Jeremy Beecham, with a sly grin, suggested that the disciplinary section of the code, as drafted, would create a great deal of employment for lawyers. Nonetheless, he ended up voting against my amendment and for the code as a whole, though he clearly knew the wording was hopelessly and dangerously ambiguous.

I rather like Jeremy Beecham. He is a fixer and manoeuvrer of the old school, a type quite distinct from the modern Millbank batch. He has been a dominant figure in Labour local government for many years, having been Leader of Newcastle City Council and now Leader of the Local Government Association (LGA). I imagine that in due course he will be appointed to the House of Lords. He is no rebel. He prefers to negotiate and apply pressure in private. On the NEC, he voted with Millbank time and time again (although on the National Policy Forum he was slightly more prepared to stick his neck out). But in the Local Government Sub-committee, he would issue coded criticisms to Hilary Armstrong, the Minister for Local Government, and he would use NEC structures to lobby on behalf of his causes. He saw himself as a representative of the interests of local government, rather than as a conduit of the views of the Labour leadership to local government. He is also a lawyer, so we had something to talk about other than Labour Party politics.

When Margaret McDonagh replied to the debate on the code,

she made a point of pouring scorn on Mark. By calling USB an "independent scrutineer", she suggested that Mark wanted a scrutineer "independent of the independent scrutineer". How many layers did Mark want? She justified the timing of the ballot – during the European election when no party would be meeting – on the grounds that Party members would be actively engaged in the European election campaign and therefore they would be enthused to vote. Our amendments were all defeated, with only the four of us voting in favour (although Sally Powell, Hilary Armstrong and Jeremy Beecham all abstained on Mark's proposal of an independent scrutineer). The code was then voted on, and passed – twice. The four of us voted against. The *Evening Standard* that afternoon predicted that the code of conduct (which it described as "draconian") would precipitate more claims of control-freakery.

Mark and Pete had put a motion on the agenda calling for trade unions to be required to ballot their members if they were to participate in electoral colleges in the future – a motion originating directly from the experience in Wales. There was much muttering from the trade unions at interference in their autonomy. Rather than have the motion voted down, Mark and Pete agreed that it would be referred to the Organisation Sub-committee. The final piece of unpleasant internal Party business was the suspension of Newark constituency Labour Party. Fiona Jones MP had been convicted of electoral fraud. She subsequently appealed and her conviction was later overturned by the Court of Appeal. There were no documents put before the NEC, but in a verbal report, Mike Penn, the National Constitutional Officer, made a number of accusations against unnamed local Party members. He claimed that the Newark constituency Labour Party was in a shambles and subject to internecine strife. He made allegations that some of the councillors had an unspecified "attitude towards planning issues" – hinting at corruption – and alleged that there had been interference with witnesses during Jones's trial. There was to be no detailed airing of the allegations or the problems, as the Party was expecting a by-election. Instead, the CLP was to be suspended forthwith. The Chair took this report and then asked if it was agreed. When we requested a vote – after all, this decision would remove rights from all the Labour Party members in the constituency, and they hadn't been heard from at all – we were asked why we would want to oppose the recommendation. The suspension was passed by nineteen votes to four – with the usual four suspects voting against.

The recommendation to suspend Newark CLP was part of Jones's own faction fight within Newark CLP – a faction fight that was enthusiastically supported by the regional full-time Party staff. Several Labour Party members had been required to give evidence during the criminal trial – and Jones was pursuing them. Newark Labour Party members were reeling. The full weight of the Party's disciplinary processes was being used in an attempt to silence Newark Labour Party members who were unhappy with Jones. In particular, one councillor, Jill Dawn (former leader of the Newark District Council), was falsely accused by Labour Party officials of receiving gifts in relation to planning applications. In fact, she had been sent some unsolicited gifts, which she had forthwith reported to the council's Chief Executive and had returned. The police had already investigated the matter and determined that she had acted impeccably. Although she had been cleared by the police, the same allegations were being made against her in Party disciplinary proceedings, instigated by the Party's regional office. The background to these allegations was that Dawn had stood against Jones in the selection for parliamentary candidate three years earlier, and Jones had never forgiven her. Rather than face a kangaroo court, Dawn resigned from the Labour Party. In the local elections in May 1999, she fought her council seat as an independent and won. She and another independent now hold the balance of power on the council. Fiona Jones was cleared in May 1999, but Newark CLP remains in a state of flux. Regional Office has gradually reactivated some of the branches, but membership has fallen away and the most active branch – the nub of the constituency – remains suspended.

Eventually, the NEC turned to the business of the forthcoming Welsh, Scottish and local elections. We were told by Millbank officials (famed for their psephological abilities) that turnout would be low because the electorate were "happy with the government". The mantra went: "the government is popular", "it is hard to motivate people to vote for what they are in favour of". Three members of the NEC commented – Jeremy Beecham complained that he and Sally Powell had not been involved in the planning for the local elections, Mary Turner (trade union representative from the GMB) cited the European Union Working Time Directive as a reason for workers to vote Labour, and Sarah Ward wanted to know how to motivate young voters – and the discussion moved on. The item on elections had taken no more than five minutes.

The next day, 24 March 1999, NATO launched its attack on Yugoslavia. The issue posed difficult challenges for the left and the response was certainly more ambiguous than it had been towards the bombing of Iraq. The Serbian atrocities in Kosova were inexcusable, as was the appalling policy of forced displacement. Some on the left, notably Ken Livingstone, Francis Wheen and Mark Seddon, argued that the crimes of the Milosevic regime justified military intervention, either by NATO or through the UN. Others on the left opposed the bombing, but called for support for the Kosova Liberation Army who were fighting for Kosovan independence. It seemed to me that the military intervention could not be supported. I could not see how the human rights abuses committed by the Milosevic regime could justify the bombing of civilians and civilian infrastructure. I also questioned NATO's motives, given its indifference to and complicity with human rights abuses elsewhere in the world. And I believe that socialists should always have an instinctive distrust of violence and militarism. Local campaigns against the war – organised by the left and the peace movement – were quickly established and I spent April and May speaking at meetings all over Britain.

Mark and I had an uneasy relationship during this period. Basil Fawlty's catchphrase, "Don't mention the war", hung over our heads. In the meantime, because of the new timetable for NEC elections, the Grassroots Alliance candidates were forced to start campaigning again – only seven months after the last election campaign had finished. When I was not speaking at meetings against the war, I was speaking at left Labour Party meetings. The war was, of course, a topic at all those meetings, as was the widespread disillusion of Party members. Very few Party members in England were actively engaged in the local election campaigns. More were taking part in Scotland and in Wales (despite their particular discontent) since the Scottish Parliament and the Welsh Assembly had been so eagerly awaited. But all over Britain, Labour Party members and Labour voters were alienated by Millbank's control-freakery and the government's Tory-like policies. On the ground, across most of the country, the Party barely functioned. Most election activity was carried out by paid Party staff, the candidates and their families. Accounts of deselection of popular councillors or Party officers after Millbank intervention were rife. The £2,000 levy on each local party was a source of complaint, especially after it turned out that if a local party could pay the lump sum, it received a 10 per cent discount, but if it asked to pay in instalments, the full £2,000 was required. Most constituency parties found it difficult enough to raise £2,000. To discover that the richer parties, who were able to pay in a lump sum, received a discount, merely added to their sense of grievance.

It was also clear from the meetings I attended that Rhodri Morgan was widely regarded as the true winner of the Welsh contest and the victim of daylight robbery. Dennis Canavan's decision to stand for election to the Scottish Parliament as an independent against the Labour Party was overwhelmingly supported by local Party members. Not so long ago, this would have been an unforgivable sin, even in the eyes of committed left-wingers, but Scottish Labour Party members had had enough. Canavan, after all, had been barred from even putting his name forward to Party members for selection. The assumption was growing that Millbank would use the same techniques against Ken Livingstone in London. The upshot of all this discontent was that Party members would resolutely fail to ring back the member lumbered with the miserable job of organising an election campaign. As I spoke at Labour Party meetings, I found myself asked more and more frequently: what was the point of staying in the

Party? What could we hope to achieve? I found it more and more difficult to respond.

In contrast, meetings outside the Labour Party were lively. On 10 April, UNISON organised a demonstration in Newcastle against low pay and for a higher minimum wage. The union had decided to hold a festival, rather than the usual political rally, at the end of the demonstration. The left organised an alternative rally after the demonstration, and speakers at it included Roger Bannister (a left member of the UNISON national executive), various UNISON activists, Sukhdev Reel, Suresh Grover (of the National Civil Rights Movement) and myself. The audience consisted of UNISON activists – low-paid public sector workers – and they were furious with the failure of the Labour government to listen to them. They were sceptical about anyone from the Labour Party – and were surprised when I attacked the government's links with big business and its failure to introduce a realistic minimum wage. I was struck by the enthusiasm of the audience, their determination to spread their campaign, in comparison with the misery and pessimism voiced at Labour Party meetings. And unlike the Labour Party meetings, there were numerous young faces in the hall.

Three weeks later, I spoke at the annual May Day rally organised by Bleanau Gwent Labour Party. Bleanau Gwent (Ebbw Vale) was once the constituency of Aneurin Bevan and Michael Foot. I was speaking with Llew Smith, the current local MP, and Peter Law, the Assembly candidate. Llew, a left-winger and member of the Campaign Group, talked about the need for the government to adopt more progressive policies. Peter Law flourished Millbank's list of the government's achievements, but got his loudest cheer when he attacked an attempt to introduce new local postcodes. After much soul-searching, I had decided to speak about the war, which was growing bloodier by the day, and I was heard out in respectful but uncertain silence. Unlike the event in Newcastle, there was little sense of enthusiasm, even though it was only four days before the first-ever Welsh elections. There were very few young people present, and a great tradition seemed to be expiring before my eyes.

Four days later, Labour lost Sheffield Council, the Rhondda and Islwyn (Neil Kinnock's former seat in South Wales and until 1999 one of the safest Labour seats in Britain). Dennis Canavan and Tommy Sheridan (candidate for the Scottish Socialist Party, famous in Scotland for being imprisoned rather than pay the poll tax) were elected to the Scottish Parliament as socialists. Labour was the single largest party in both the Scottish Parliament and the Welsh Assembly, but had no overall majority in either. The clear beneficiaries of the decline in the Labour vote were Plaid Cymru and the Scottish National Party. In Scotland, Labour entered into coalition with the Liberals. Alun Michael in Wales chose to tough it out alone.

The NEC met three weeks later, on 25 May. The Chair opened the meeting by saying we had had "successful" Welsh and Scottish elections. Blair spoke, and called the local, Scottish and Welsh elections a "remarkably good result for a mid-term election". The problems, as he saw them, were with Labour Party structures or local leaders. He returned to his old theme, that Labour Party supporters complained that the government had not gone far enough. He ended by attacking MPs, saying they should be "not just a pressure group for government, they are also ambassadors for the government". Margaret McDonagh took an even more robust approach. Declaring that there was "a good result in Scotland", she went on to blame the Scottish Labour Party members for their lack of technical skills. "I would be surprised if anyone in Scotland knew what a 'reading pad' was. There's a poor culture in Scotland, it's similar to London in the 1980s." (As an activist in London in the 1980s, I can assure McDonagh that we all knew perfectly well what a reading pad was – an essential electoral tool.) Vernon Hince (now re-elected as RMT Deputy General Secretary) complained, but only after Blair had left, that he was disappointed that the Prime Minister had blamed local activists. And that was the extent of the discussion at Labour's NEC of these historic election results. The subsequent minutes record McDonagh as saying "the Scottish result was a testament to the Labour Party working at its best".

During the meeting, Blair seemed determined to reiterate that everything the government did was right. He referred to the "significant rebellion on incapacity benefit" but insisted "these were the right proposals". Sixty-five Labour MPs had voted against the government's proposals to restrict access to incapacity benefit, and to alter its status from a universal benefit to a means-tested benefit. Blair said that the government's abolition of legal aid, the imposition of vouchers on asylum seekers and introduction of performance-related pay for teachers (all going through the House of Commons at the time) were also "the right proposals". There was some muted criticism from Diana Holland on incapacity benefit and from Sally Powell on asylum seekers. Both questions were phrased in a low-key way, and I was saddened to see how obviously nervous both of them were at voicing even the most muted criticisms of government policy. On the war in Yugoslavia, Pete Willsman and I complained about the use of cluster bombs and the reported use of depleted uranium against the civilian population. Cluster bombs are banned by the Geneva Convention. Depleted uranium is said to have caused a huge increase in the incidence of cancer and leukaemia wherever it has been used. In a brief interjection, Michael Cashman disparaged "so-called innocent civilians". Blair's response was "don't believe all you read in the newspapers". Other members of .the NEC supported the military action with some enthusiasm and praised the Prime Minister's widely televised visit to the Albanian refugee camps. He joked: "At least I'll be popular in Albania." It has now been confirmed that depleted uranium and cluster bombs were used extensively by NATO forces in Yugoslavia, at terrible and as yet unknown human cost to the people on the ground who have to live with the mess we created. I don't know whether, when he answered our questions at the NEC, Blair did or did not know the truth about the use of cluster bombs and depleted uranium. I got the impression, frankly, that he really didn't care one way or another.

For Millbank, the real business of this NEC meeting was to approve the proposals to put the Labour Party's membership department out to private tender, and it got this under way even before Blair had arrived for the meeting. Presenting the proposals was a member of Party staff – Fiona Gordon, then working in Margaret McDonagh's office, and now regional director of the Labour Party in the West Midlands. She was giving a Powerpoint presentation – full of up-to-the-minute techno-talk. The blinds were drawn, the room was in half darkness and everyone was facing this young woman and her display screen. She was going through the slides and making her points crisply and competently. Suddenly, however, her face was transfigured by an expression of delight and awe, and she seemed to lose all focus. As we turned around to see what had derailed such a well-prepared recitation, we saw Blair making his way towards his seat. He waved, somewhat self-deprecatingly, and invited the besotted Gordon to "carry on" and not to mind him. You would have thought the Messiah had appeared.

As Pete Willsman had predicted, the feasibility study commissioned in January and carried out by KPMG had recommended that the Party's membership records should be administered by a private company, rather than in-house. Problems with membership touch a nerve amongst Party activists. Ever since the membership department was centralised in the early 1990s, there had been complaints about its inefficiency. The question was whether the administration could be improved in-house or not. As the discussion developed, it became clear that there had been a lack of investment in technology in the membership department in the last few years. The four of us, and the GMB, voiced concerns about the proposed "outsourcing": lack of confidentiality, lack of guarantees for the staff currently working in the membership department, and the fact that a large City firm would become privy to Labour's membership records. Told by Dianne Hayter that all organisations contract these functions out nowadays, Mark Seddon responded that *Tribune* would certainly not contemplate letting its subscription list go outside the newspaper. A private tender was agreed, but with six voting against: ourselves and the two GMB members. This was the highest number of NEC members to vote against a Millbank recommendation in my two years on the NEC.

There was an intriguing little scrap over the House of Lords. At the previous meeting, in March, we had been informed that the Party's submissions to the Wakeham Commission on the House of Lords was due a month later and that Professor Keith Ewing, besides apparently conducting a review of Party finances, would also be co-ordinating the submission on the Lords. Ewing told the NEC that submissions to him on this subject would have to be made within two weeks. He promised to conduct meetings with Party members around the country. When, at the end of April, the Party's submission to the House of Lords was press-released, it included, to the shock of many Party members, a proposal for a wholly appointed second chamber. I kicked myself for not having asked for a discussion at the NEC in March, or at the very least for not having put down a marker in favour of a directly elected second chamber (an idea that commands wide support among Party members, as does outright abolition of a second chamber). In response to the announcement of the Party's submission, I wrote a letter to the *Guardian* attacking a wholly appointed second chamber, and making it clear that this "official" submission had never been approved by the NEC or any other Labour Party body. At the May NEC, it became obvious that a number of other members – not exclusively the Grassroots Alliance – had kicked themselves too. Dianne Hayter said that, although she agreed with the contents of the submission, it should have come before the NEC first. Mary Turner said that the NEC could have been recalled to discuss the submission. I backed them both up. In response, McDonagh claimed that the newspapers had reported the Ewing submission before it had been published and that she was not responsible for what was in the press.

At the end of the meeting, Pete and I proposed a motion to give a further right of appeal to would-be Labour candidates who had been excluded from the panel for the Greater London Assembly. Of the 230 applicants, only 94 had been accepted. The others, principally but not exclusively from the left, were deemed inappropriate in a variety of ways. Left-wingers, including Christine Shawcroft (councillor for twelve years, member of the London Labour Party Board, primary school teacher and mother), Geoff Martin (twenty years a UNISON activist, previously a Labour councillor, convenor of London Health Emergency, convenor of London UNISON Affiliated Political Fund, football supporter and father) and Theresa Pearce (voted by Labour Party members onto the Party's National Constitutional Committee in two successive years) were told that they lacked "life experience". A high proportion of black candidates had been excluded, including Kumar Murshid (councillor in Tower Hamlets), Raj Jethwa (ethnic minorities officer to the London Labour Party) and Peter Herbert (chair of the Society of Black Lawyers). There had been a limited right of appeal, but different procedures had been applied to different candidates. Some had attended a further interview; others had simply indicated that they wished to appeal and then received a letter in response informing them that their appeal had been unsuccessful. Clive Soley argued that Pete and I were wrong to put forward any motion on this subject: "this motion falls into the mistake of trying to govern organisation by motions". As Chair of the London selection panel (which had made the decisions), he defended the selection process on the grounds that it encouraged equal opportunities; he also noted that the selection panel had asked all the candidates whether the process was fair – and at that time not one had complained. Anne Begg (an MP and also a member of the selection board, although not a Londoner) backed him up, saying that a decision that a candidate was "lacking in life experience didn't mean that you were lacking in life experience, it meant that you must fill that part of the form in". She never commented on why an inability to fill in that part of the form had afflicted left-wingers, but not Blairites. Our motion was defeated by fourteen votes to four.

Mark's and Pete's motion stipulating that in future Party contests trade unions could only participate if they balloted their members had been well and truly kicked into the long grass. Mark had attended the Organisation Sub-committee (the most important sub-committee of the NEC, where significant management decisions concerning the Party were made; Pete was a member). There he and Pete had listened to the trade unions complaining for an hour that the pair of them were trying to interfere with their autonomy. Clive Soley then proposed what he called a compromise: that there should be a review of voting arrangements. Pete was asked if he would withdraw his motion in support of Soley's compromise. Pete asked in reply what the actual wording of Soley's compromise would be. The Chair refused to allow Soley to read out his wording until Pete had said whether or not he would withdraw the original motion. In the absence of any alternative wording to consider, Pete refused to withdraw the motion; it was put to the vote and defeated with only Pete voting in favour. We never heard from Soley the terms of the compromise he was proposing.

At the end of the May NEC meeting, the guest list for Annual Conference was approved. As usual, amongst the guests to be invited were the diplomatic representatives of just about every country recognised by the UK. Millbank proposed that all ambassadors, save those representing Sudan, Serbia and Burma, be invited. These three were to be excluded on the grounds of their regimes' records on human rights and democracy. Iraq would also be excluded, because it has no diplomatic relations with the UK. I proposed that the Indonesian ambassador should also be excluded, given the human rights abuses and lack of democracy in Indonesia. My proposal was dismissed out of hand on the grounds that Indonesia was moving towards democracy and its ambassador simply must be invited.

The headlines the following day were: "Blair warns welfare rebels" (*Guardian*) and "Blair orders MPs to stop whingeing" (*Independent*). These articles were spun out of just one sentence uttered by Blair, seemingly apropos of very little, in the course of a lengthy commentary on a variety of subjects. The actual business of the meeting went unreported.

On 10 June came the European elections, and another poor result for New Labour. Party members had been on strike throughout the campaign, partly as a result of election burn-out (most parties outside London had to fight the May local government, Scottish Parliament or Welsh Assembly elections as well as the European elections), but mainly because of discontent with both the government and Millbank. From sixty-two members of the European Parliament, Labour was reduced to twenty-nine. In the Leeds Central by-election, a safe Labour seat, Hilary Benn retained the seat for Labour, but on a turnout of 19.6 per cent – the lowest since the Second World War – and Labour's majority fell from 20,689 to 2,293. Labour's core voters had stayed away from the polls in droves.

On 22 June, the NEC result was announced. The ballot had closed a week earlier, but we had all been required to sign pledges that we had no complaints about its conduct before the result would be announced. The Grassroots Alliance lost one seat – Pete Willsman's – although our share of the vote actually increased. (Lord) Tom Sawyer, standing on the Millbank-backed Members First slate, topped the poll. Mark, myself and Christine Shawcroft were second, third and fourth respectively, followed by Michael Cashman and Diana Jeuda. The turnout was far lower than the previous year, the election having been conducted by Millbank in near secrecy.

Millbank had achieved their principal aims: they had kept the election quiet, retained Cashman's and Jeuda's seats and turned out one of us. Their strategy now was to befuddle the members with (relatively) famous names, following on from Cashman's 1998 success. In 1999, Sawyer was widely known as the party's former General Secretary, and a long-time senior trade unionist. But the post-1997 restructuring of the NEC, Millbank's own contrivance, posed an embarrassing problem for Sawyer. The new Constituency Labour Parties section of the NEC had been designed specifically to exclude parliamentarians. Sawyer was a Labour member of the House of Lords and hence a member of the Parliamentary Labour Party and therefore, it might have been assumed, ineligible to stand. What's more, Cashman had just been elected a member of the European Parliament – also included within the definition of parliamentarians. When the "Partnership in Power" proposals were discussed at the NEC in 1997, the NEC had been specifically assured that the exclusions from the CLP section would encompass MPs, Lords and MEPs. However, since the rule as finally drafted did not contain a specific reference to members of the House of Lords, Sawyer was ruled an eligible candidate. We had anticipated that, and indeed had wondered whether other celebrity members of the House of Lords would be approached by Millbank to stand. Quite why the former General Secretary of the Party and peer of the realm should want to submit himself for election to the constituency section of the Labour NEC still remains a mystery to me. During his first year of office, Sawyer attended only four of the seven NEC meetings and none of the National Policy Forum meetings. I never heard him open his mouth at any of the NEC meetings.

Cashman's position was even more controversial. An MEP was obviously excluded under the rule from standing in the constituency section – it was not a question of whether the rule had been badly drafted or whether the spirit of "Partnership in Power" would be infringed. MEPs were explicitly excluded from that section and indeed had their own NEC representatives. Millbank decided that the relevant date determining whether or not somebody was eligible to stand in a particular section was not the date of the election, or the date of taking office, but the date of nomination as a candidate. Thus, on 9 April 1999 (when nominations closed), Cashman was an "ordinary" member, though everybody knew that he would almost certainly be a sitting MEP by the time the results were announced. He was elected to the European Parliament on 12 June 1999 and elected to the NEC as an "ordinary" member on 22 June 1999. His term of office as a constituency NEC member commenced in October 1999 and ran for a year. Thus, for the whole of his year of office (October 1999 to October 2000), ostensibly representing ordinary members, Cashman was an MEP. In my view, that infringed not only the spirit of "Partnership in Power" but also the actual rule itself.

Losing Pete Willsman, and all his expertise and experience, definitely hurt, especially since he had fallen victim to Millbank's playing fast and loose on the eligibility of candidates for the CLP section. Nonetheless, although the Grassroots Alliance lost one seat, our share of the vote went up from 46.38 per cent in 1998 to 47.7 per cent. Christine's election was sweet revenge for her exclusion from the panel of candidates for the Greater London Asssembly elections – Labour Party members had voted for her despite her alleged "lack of life experience".

5

The Demented Octopus

Since the election victory of 1997, the fashioning of Labour Party policy has been the responsibility of the National Policy Forum, set up by "Partnership in Power" at that year's conference. Ken Livingstone once described its tangled lines of accountability as resembling "a demented octopus". After two years of intensive engagement with this body, I can confirm the simile. It proved a futile battle with a monster with many hands governed by a single head.

The National Policy Forum consists of 175 "delegates", although not all of them are elected. Of these, 72 represent constituencies or regions. They are elected at annual or regional conferences by constituency delegates. There are 30 delegates from the trade unions, including delegates from all the major affiliated unions. There are also 9 delegates from local government (Labour councillors), 7 from the socialist societies, 2 from the Co-Operative Party, 15 from the MPs and MEPs, and 8 appointed by the cabinet or shadow cabinet. Among these are some of the government's most senior members: in 1998–99 Blair, Prescott, Gordon Brown, Jack Straw, Stephen Byers, David Blunkett, Robin Cook and Frank Dobson were appointed. Members of the National Executive Committee are also automatically members of the National Policy Forum. Of the 175 participants in the NPF, only 78 (including the six constituency seats on the NEC) represent individual Party members.

Many of the National Policy Forum participants have a direct interest in retaining the government's patronage. For many of the constituency delegates, it is a stepping stone in their career advancement. Of the 72 constituency delegates in 1999–2000, 23 found places on the Party's National Parliamentary Panel. Time and time again, most National Policy Forum delegates loyally voted for the Millbank line.

The National Policy Forum was supposed to produce policy by consensus rather than resolution. The argument was that back in the bad old days, delegates to Conference were confronted with composited resolutions. Parts of those resolutions would reflect policy on which a local delegate was mandated; other parts might not. The composites themselves had been achieved by a process of amalgamating all the motions put in on a particular topic into two, or three, differing positions. In the process of compositing, deals were done, crucial issues could be lost and strange alliances made to assist or wreck a proposal. The champions of "Partnership in Power" claimed the new National Policy Forum would put an end to deal-making behind closed doors. In reality, it has reduced the policy-making process to one exclusively shaped by deals done behind closed doors.

The National Policy Forum meets in secret. Its deliberations are not open to the media or to Party members (unlike annual conferences), although a number of observers from the Prime Minister's office or the Downing Street policy unit sit in. Reports of the proceedings are issued in heavily edited form by Millbank and cannot be challenged or corrected by participants. All discussions must follow the two-year "rolling programme" of topics designated by Millbank. In 1998 and 1999, it was health; welfare; and crime and justice; in 1999 and 2000, education and employment; democracy and citizenship; the economy; industry, agriculture, and culture; the environment, transport, and the regions; and "Britain in the World". "Europe" was discussed over a one-year cycle in 1998, as a manifesto had to be in place for the 1999 European elections.

Draft documents on each topic were produced by Millbank and circulated to local parties. Local parties were then encouraged to hold a forum on one of the designated topics. Most local parties restricted themselves, of necessity, to only one or two of the year's topics. These local forums tended to be attended by around forty people (roughly the same number of local activists who attend constituency general committee meetings). No votes were taken at the forums. No motions were considered. Discussions were held mainly in workshop style, and a facilitator took notes of some of the suggestions made. These notes were then sent to Millbank. What happened to them there seemed largely a matter of the political priorities of Millbank and 10 Downing Street. There was no mechanism of any kind whereby local parties or individual members could chase up their input.

Overseeing this process were nine policy commissions, one for each topic. The policy commissions met in private and on an *ad hoc* basis. "Whenever Frank Dobson has a spare half hour" was one description of the timetable for the health policy commission. If minutes exist for these meetings, they have never been circulated. The membership of the policy commissions was divided into three blocks of three seats each. Three were appointed from the NEC – usually trade union representatives. Three were appointed from the National Policy Forum – a trade union representative, a constituency representative (elected by the constituency representatives to the National Policy Forum) and an MP. Three were then appointed by government, including usually the relevant cabinet ministers. Thus, the Policy Commission on "Britain in the World" in 1998 consisted of Robin Cook, George Robertson (then Secretary of State for Defence) and Clare Short from the government, Diana Holland, John Hannett and Anne Picking (all trade union representatives) from the NEC, Jim Knight, David Martin MEP and John Edmonds (GMB General Secretary) from the National Policy Forum. Of those nine, only one represents ordinary Party members (and is now a prospective parliamentary candidate) and he was elected to the policy commission by the National Policy Forum majority as Millbank's favoured candidate. Thus the body that was supposed to inform government policy with the views of Party members was dominated by the very people who were making and implementing government policy in the first place.

At the apex of the process sat a Joint Policy Commission, which assembled at Downing Street on an *ad hoc* basis. Its membership included the Prime Minister and Deputy Prime Minister and seven other cabinet members. There were also eight representatives from the NEC, including Ian McCartney MP (effectively another government representative), and three National Policy Forum members, among them yet another on-message MP – Mike Gapes – and Bill Morris of the TGWU. There is only one representative who does not have a senior labour movement position, but even she is yet another safe pair of hands: a National Policy Forum member, a member of the National Parliamentary Panel, paid assistant to a Labour MP and another prospective parliamentary candidate.

The draft documents were written by Millbank policy officers, theoretically under the supervision of the relevant policy commission, and presented to the National Policy Forum, which met two or three times a year and was conducted in the same vein as the local policy forums. Unlike the local forums, every once in a while there would be a vote at the National Policy Forum. According to "Partnership in Power" at the end of the two-year rolling process the National Policy Forum would be asked to vote on a final document on each topic. Those documents would then be put to Conference, where they would be voted on as a whole. There would be no opportunity for conference delegates to propose amendments to the documents. However, amendments reflecting "minority positions" would be put to Conference if they had mustered the support of a minimum number of National Policy Forum delegates. When "Partnership in Power" was passed in October 1997, Conference was assured that on major policy differences, there would be "majority" and "minority" positions on which delegates could vote. In this way, it was claimed, Conference itself would continue to decide the crucial policy questions, if not the detail.

At the March 1999 NEC, it was decided that the threshold for a "minority position" at the National Policy Forum to reach the conference agenda would be 35 delegates or 25 per cent of those present at the National Policy Forum, whichever was the greater number. Conspiracy theorists amongst us wondered whether the figure of 35 had been arrived at after an article in

Tribune by Pete Willsman had referred to Grassroots Alliance membership of the National Policy Forum being in the region of 30.

The first full meeting of the National Policy Forum I attended was in January 1999 in Swansea. No decisions were made. We sat around in workshops, brainstorming on the policy documents. A Millbank official took notes in each workshop. At the end of each session, the official read back his or her notes. Many of the suggestions made by Grassroots Alliance representatives failed to find their way into these notes. At the end of each workshop, we would therefore patiently repeat the points we had made and insist that they were included. Millbank officials would then summarise the points made in the various workshops to a full meeting of the National Policy Forum. Again, most of the points made by the Grassroots Alliance, which we had assiduously ensured were included in the notes, somehow failed to find their way into the reports to the full meeting. We would stand up and insist that the points were put back in.

The first voting meeting of the National Policy Forum was held in Durham on the weekend of 2–4 July 1999. On the table were the three "first-year" policy documents: on health, crime and justice, and welfare. Submissions on those three topics from policy forums, constituency parties, trade unions and individuals had been circulated to all members of the National Policy Forum. However, the only way points made in the submissions could actually be raised in debate was if they were redrafted as formal amendments by a National Policy Forum delegate and then backed by at least eight other delegates. However, unless a topic was specifically raised in the submissions, it could not be brought up by National Policy Forum delegates, no matter how many of us wanted to raise it. We were given just under two weeks to read all the submissions, to draft amendments and to obtain the agreement of eight other delegates.

The main thrust of all the documents was to trumpet the success of the government. Small achievements, such as the introduction of NHS Direct, were referred to over and over again. Another aim was to sell government policies to discontented

Labour Party members and trade unionists. Various methods were used to this end. One was simply omitting mention of the problematic policy altogether. There was, for example, no reference in the crime and justice consultation document to the government's plans to remove the right of defendants to choose jury trial. Alternatively, government policy might be written using language that Party members were expected to relate to. Thus, the abolition of legal aid for personal injury cases was described as "targeting on those people who are most in need of help, and on high-priority cases". Most recipients of the document did not know that this was code for the withdrawal of legal aid, and most of those who did were opposed to the idea. Their submissions were ignored by the Crime and Justice Policy Commission.

The documents also attempted to diffuse potential rebellions amongst Labour Party members by dodging key issues and hoping that Party members would not raise them. Low pay in the NHS is something many Party members feel strongly about. But when, in its first draft, the health policy document listed five reasons why the NHS had difficulty recruiting or retaining staff, pay rates were not among them. Sometimes there were hints that the government was going to take on board major worries of Party members. For example, nine out of ten of the submissions on the welfare document wanted to restore the link between pensions and earnings. In response, the policy document stated: "over the longer term our aim is that it [the minimum income guarantee] should rise in line with earnings". But this statement remained wholly at odds with government policy, and was merely a sop.

The Grassroots Alliance National Policy Forum representatives submitted formal amendments to the three documents. On welfare, we opposed the government's proposals to means-test incapacity benefit, and supported the restoration of the link between pensions and earnings, and the restoration of welfare benefits to asylum seekers; we also called for the retention of housing benefit (ominously referred to in the document as needing reform to strike "a better balance between tenants' rights and responsibilities"), the reinstatement of rent controls, and an increase in the upper earnings limits on national insurance contributions so that marginal rates of taxation were equalised between rich and poor. On health, we called for local accountability of representatives on NHS trusts, opposition to Private Finance Initiative deals and an increase in health workers' pay. On crime and justice, our amendments called for a greater emphasis on tackling poverty as a cause of crime, on community-oriented sentences, on retaining legal aid for personal injury cases, and the right of a defendant to choose trial by jury. I was charged with drafting the amendments on crime and justice and at the last minute I decided to add a call for the abolition of wigs and gowns in Court (something referred to in the submissions). I thought that here was an issue that was not likely to be subject to a predetermined New Labour line, and we might be able to have a real debate on it.

We were hopeful that we could build alliances on a number of issues, so that at last some criticisms of New Labour's policies might get aired at Party Conference. UNISON, the GMB and MSF had all made submissions or proposed amendments calling for a restoration of the link between pensions and earnings (in line with their union policies) and for paid, rather than unpaid, parental leave. They had all criticised the abolition of incapacity benefit. The unions were also calling for an increase in employment rights, for a minimum level of income for those who cannot work, and for increases in child benefit. On health, they wanted more effective health and safety legislation, and implementation of the Royal Commission report on long-term care (including the abolition of charges in residential nursing homes). On the more contentious health issues, however, the unions restricted themselves to coded suggestions. UNISON's amendment said only that NHS "pay and the pay system must be fair and equitable for all staff and centrally funded". No union took a stance against the Private Finance Initiative – even though several unions had policies opposing it. All UNISON would ask for was that "Labour will ensure that PFI deals promote the interest of the NHS and all its staff, prevent privatisation of services and safeguard quality". On crime and justice, UNISON called for adequate access to justice for all, and noted that unemployment, low pay, poor skills and bad housing create conditions for crime. I therefore expected

UNISON to support our amendment on tackling poverty in order to reduce crime.

When delegates arrived at Durham station on the Friday afternoon, we found that minibuses had been laid on to take us to the university, where the National Policy Forum was to meet. I had caught the same London train as most of the members of Millbank staff and I ended up in the same minibus as several of them, including Margaret McDonagh. As we drove through Durham, McDonagh said, "Didn't Tony go to school here?" I nearly said, "Tony who?"

When we arrived at the university, we were told that all those who had proposed an amendment would soon be informed whether the relevant policy commission had accepted the amendment or not. If an amendment was accepted, the wording of the policy document would be changed accordingly before it was put to the vote on Sunday. If it was not accepted, the proposer of the amendment had to attend a private meeting, described as a "one-to-one" with the relevant minister, to talk through the amendment. We were entitled to bring one "supporter" but not all eight delegates who had seconded the amendment. In the meeting, the proposer would have to decide, alone and without consultation, whether to accept any rewording or compromises or to withdraw altogether. If the proposer did not accept the compromises, or agree to withdraw, the amendment would be put to the vote at the plenary session of the National Policy Forum on the Sunday morning.

Given the composition and methods of the National Policy Forum, we never expected anything but an uphill struggle that weekend in Durham. Our best hope was to secure sufficient votes – 35 or 25 per cent of those present – to get some of our amendments to Conference to be voted on as "minority" positions. Even the most jaundiced amongst us, however, did not expect that just keeping the amendments before the National Policy Forum, and insisting that they were put to a vote, would prove an all-out battle in itself.

At the appointed time, Ray Davison (a delegate from the South West region) and I showed up outside the small building in which the "one to one" sessions were being held, waiting for our chance to discuss some of the crime and justice amendments. Sessions were being held simultaneously on all three policy topics, and the proposers of various amendments stood around outside the building because there was nowhere to wait. One chair had been brought outside and we took turns sitting on it. Somebody came out of the crime and justice session to thank us for arriving and to say that they were running late. We waited. As we waited, various messages kept coming out of the welfare meeting. Alistair Darling and Angela Eagle were trying to get the Grassroots Alliance to withdraw all of its amendments. The trade unions were said to be huddling in corners.

As Ray and I walked into our "one-to-one" (after an hour and a half's wait), there were at least ten people sitting round the table, including Home Office Minister Paul Boateng, Colin Pickthall MP (parliamentary private secretary to Jack Straw), two people from the Downing Street policy office, an adviser to Jack Straw, Margaret Wall (Vice-Chair of the National Policy Forum) and a Millbank policy officer. The late and deeply missed Audrey Wise, from the Conference Arrangements Committee, sat in as an observer (and a welcome friendly face). We were told that only one of my amendments – on domestic violence – would be accepted. Boateng and I then engaged in a long argument over two other amendments. My amendment referred to poverty being one of the causes of crime. Boateng said that the philosophy behind this proposition might be in line with a strand of Labour Party opinion, but it was not his view. After forty-five minutes, I refused to withdraw either that proposition or a second amendment on learning the lessons from the Stephen Lawrence inquiry. I was dreading the prospect of going through the same lengthy exercise with my remaining ten amendments, so I was relieved when Margaret Wall announced that all these amendments would be debated and put to the vote on Sunday. That was really all Ray and I had ever wanted.

Outside I found that other Grassroots Alliance delegates had been subjected to a similar exercise for much longer periods, in the case of Ann Black (responsible for the bulk of Grassroots

Alliance amendments on welfare) for over four hours. Faced with pressure from government ministers, who were willing to drown ordinary delegates with facts and figures, some of the Grassroots Alliance amendments had been withdrawn, or accepted in rewritten and usually anodyne form. We had no idea what had happened to the rest of the amendments, in particular to the trade union amendments.

The next morning all became clear. All of the trade unions' amendments on welfare had been withdrawn in favour of a broad composite drawn up by the TGWU. The composite promised a "review of the welfare state". No timescale was given for the review, no parameters were proposed, and the mechanics of the thing were hazy at best. The welfare policy commission was delighted to accept the review, and made great play of it, claiming that there was now no need for any of our amendments on welfare to be debated or voted upon, because they could all be submitted to the review. It was a shabby deal, and the trade union representatives who signed up to it badly let down their own members and their own unions' policy commitments. All the other amendments submitted by delegates had either been neutered or withdrawn. Only the Grassroots Alliance amendments were left to be debated.

We spent the whole of Saturday in workshops of some twenty people. Each workshop was supposed to discuss all the amendments, but inevitably most discussion centred on the dissident amendments from the Grassroots Alliance, as all the others had been compromised or withdrawn. The composition of the workshops had been decided in advance by Millbank, and there were no more than two or three Grassroots Alliance delegates in each workshop. I was alone in mine. Each workshop was attended by a government minister delegated to discuss the specific topic. In addition, each workshop had at least one other government minister posted in it throughout proceedings, presumably to keep an eye on the rest of us. MPs and ministers were well briefed. They complained that our amendments were, variously, too long, too short, not specific enough or too specific, and, most unacceptably, "inconsistent with government policy". Nonetheless, some delegates offered support for some of our positions, princi-pally on legal aid, trial by jury, pensions and universal benefits. (The amendment on restoring welfare benefits to asylum seekers had been ruled out of order by Millbank – on the grounds that it was not relevant to welfare.) Other delegates argued that, although they did not agree with the amendments themselves, there was no doubt they represented genuine concerns among Party members and should therefore be put to Conference as minority positions for debate and final decision. That was, after all, what had been promised in "Partnership in Power".

On the Saturday evening in Durham a dinner was held. These occasions are used by MPs and ministers to network among trade union and constituency delegates. The trade union delegates use them to lobby ministers. Constituency delegates are generally flattered by the experience of chatting away to a government minister. As a number of people associated with the Grassroots Alliance sat down at a table, other delegates moved self-consciously away, apparently fearing contagion. Diana Jeuda, approaching me at the end of the dinner, told me that she should not be seen talking to me – and then wanted to know how many votes I thought there were for the Grassroots Alliance amend-ments due to be debated the next morning. Millbank officials were wandering around making sure everyone knew what was expected of them tomorrow – and again, giving us a wide berth. Later that evening, I put together two-minute speeches proposing each of my crime and justice amendments. I was well aware that all the amendments would be defeated – the question was whether we would cross the threshold and get them put before Conference.

Of the 175 delegates to the National Policy Forum, only 90 bothered to attend the next morning's crucial voting session – one of the very rare occasions when one's presence at the National Policy Forum might actually mean something. So we needed 35 votes – 40 per cent of the total present. The welfare discussion was first, and featured Alistair Darling speaking for twenty minutes. He followed a standard New Labour pattern. First, jokes are made about the speaker's radical past – Darling referred to speaking at Labour Party Conference twenty years earlier in support of nationalising the top 200 monopolies (Militant Tendency policy, instantly recognisable to everybody in the room). Then there was a deprecating reference to the old ways of policy making by resolutions at Conference. Then the meat of the speech was devoted to soundbite rebuttals of each of the amendments to be voted on. After Darling, we were treated to a general "report from workshops" – in which one of the trusted delegates would outline why the majority of delegates were opposed to the Grassroots Alliance amendments. Ann Black and the other Grassroots Alliance proposers of welfare amendments were all ready with detailed arguments, but there was to be no further discussion and no more speeches were permitted. Suddenly, we moved straight to a vote on each of our amendments. I looked round the hall to see all of the trade unions present voting against restoring the link between pensions and earnings, against defence of incapacity benefit, against restoration of rent controls, against increasing some national insurance contributions for the rich, etcetera. Delegates who in the workshops had supported our positions, or at least had felt that the amendments should be aired at Conference, now put up their hands to vote down our amendments. The highest vote we achieved in the welfare section was 12: for a fairer distribution of national insurance contributions.

The crime and justice session followed the same pattern. Boateng kicked off with the predictable joke about his radical past, then embarked on a diatribe about a single mother, living high up in a tower block, scared to go out in case her flat was burgled or her toddler contracted a disease from used syringes left lying about by local junkies. The relevance to our particular amendments was unclear. He then went through the various amendments, indicating that he and I could have compromised on some of them (although no such compromise had been offered to me). He sought to diffuse any potential rebellion over legal aid by saying that it was only to be withdrawn in cases of personal injury caused by negligence, giving the clear impression that negligence represented a minority of personal injury cases – rather than, as it does, the overwhelming majority of such cases. He was

followed by a pre-programmed workshop reporter. I had no
opportunity to speak, not even to correct Boateng's misrepresentation of our discussion. The amendments were defeated one by
one. I was glad, though, to see Jeremy Beecham vote with us on
trial by jury and legal aid. On these two amendments we achieved
16 votes, our highest tally of the day. Even the amendment
proposing the abolition of wigs and gowns was subject to heavy
Millbank whipping and was voted down by the same overwhelming majority as the rest. There was only one amendment to the
health document – calling for the accountability of local decision
makers in the NHS to their local community. This too was voted
down. Altogether, the votes took no more than twenty minutes.
On several occasions, the Chair, Ian McCartney MP, did not even
bother to look up as he announced that an amendment was
defeated.

The whole weekend felt like a waste. For all our efforts, all our
detailed preparations, all our moderation and conciliation, we
had emerged empty-handed. Had our amendments been subject
to a one member, one vote referendum among Party members,
most would, without doubt, have received solid majority support.
Now, these positions – and, more important, the broad ideals they
embodied – would not even appear on the Party's annual conference agenda. Conference would be presented with all the Millbank policy documents on a take-it-or-leave-it basis, which meant
it had been reduced to a rubber stamp for the leadership. Most
distressingly, I had witnessed virtually all the trade union delegates
abandon their members' clearly stated policies and priorities in
exchange for substanceless assurances from Millbank.

In its story on the National Policy Forum, the *Observer* reported:
"Ministers and Downing Street policy advisers put intense pressure on left-wing activists yesterday to drop their amendments. A
delegate described the procedure as 'really Orwellian'. Another
said: 'It was reminiscent of the worst back-stage manoeuvring at a
party conference. They wanted all minority positions withdrawn.'"
The official view, revealed in a report sent out by South East
constituency delegates and also, identically worded save for the
name of the region and delegates, by West Midlands delegates,

was that: "six out of 175 delegates only supported some [amend-ments]. This reflected the consensual nature of the process, the success of the consultation and the hard work of ministers in explaining the implication of policies to delegates." In reports fed to the press, Ann Black and I were accused of "holding the Forum to ransom" because we had refused to withdraw our amendments and insisted on a vote.

As for the much-vaunted "review on welfare" for which the trade unions gave away so much, it has not been seen or heard of since. Social Security Minister Alistair Darling is said to have conducted meetings around the country, but no documents were drawn up, there were no requests for submissions, there was no publicity and no timetable.

6

"It Is a Rule, But It Is Not
Written Down"

Electoral setbacks posed a thorny problem for New Labour. After all, victory at the ballot box had always been its trump card, and its answer to all criticisms. And for Labour Party members who had experienced the long and bitter years of opposition, Blair's ability to deliver such victories was a powerful attraction. So when the electorate began misbehaving in the spring of 1999, Millbank's only response was to blame the members – it simply could not afford to concede that its methods cost not only principles, but also votes.

At the National Executive Committee's Local Government Subcommittee on 28 June 1999, Hilary Armstrong, Minister for Local Government and one of the three government representatives on the NEC, argued that the recent results showed that Labour voters were "very discerning" in that they refused to vote Labour in areas where the local Labour council was "bad" – apparently, meaning either incompetent or corrupt. This seemed something of a sweeping generalisation. I had not heard Sheffield under Labour denounced as either corrupt or incompetent, yet we had lost Sheffield. In Wales, councillors in Bleanau Gwent had been convicted of criminal offences, yet we retained Bleanau Gwent and lost the Rhondda and Islwyn. Rather than intervening in Doncaster, New Labour had happily defended councillors who had been convicted of criminal offences, whilst attempting to smear Ron Rose, the whistle-blower. Responding to Armstrong, Graham Lane (Local Government Association spokesperson on education) exploded: "I hope I never see a Labour spokesperson saying that the reason people didn't vote is that they are too happy with the government." New Labour spin was not going down well with seasoned local government operators. They were being blamed for Labour voters deserting the government and they resented it.

As I went into the NEC on 27 July, the BBC asked me about a Millbank document on the recent elections. They told me that this would be the main item of discussion at the meeting. I had to admit that, like most other NEC members, but unlike the journalists, I'd not been given any advance sight of the paper. When I read it inside the meeting, I found that, according to Millbank's analysis, the Party's greatest result was in the Eddisbury by-election – which Labour had lost. Margaret Beckett, attending the NEC as the Party's campaign co-ordinator for the summer elections, described the elections as a "mixed bag of results". The European results, however, were acknowledged to be disappoint-ing. The lessons drawn were as follows: the electorate as a whole could not be taken for granted, the Tories were able to motivate their core vote, there was a lack of interest in Europe amongst the voters, and (according to Margaret McDonagh) a lack of campaigning ability among Party members, particularly in safe seats. The recommendations included a Party-wide consultation on changes to the electoral system, a request to the government to hold local and European elections on the same dates in future, and another consultation on "whether local Party structures are suitable for current campaigning demands and whether there is a need to reform and modernise them". This was code for the abolition of the remaining democratic decision-making forums in local parties and later became the main thrust of something called "The 21st Century Party" consultation document.

This time, it was not just the Grassroots Alliance taking issue with Millbank's analysis. Pauline Green (who had been re-elected to the European Parliament from London and who, less than three months later, was to resign her seat as an MEP) was clearly furious at having been trivialised in the European election leaf-lets. She complained, "We were asked for small biographies, but we didn't expect those to be the only descriptions of us on the leaflet. I am now known all over London as a Dusty Springfield and *Star Trek* fan. I would have preferred something about my politics as well." Alan Donnelly criticised the multi-member electoral system for European elections and wanted to retain the constituency link. Jeremy Beecham referred to a drift away from the Labour Party in Scotland and Wales, and Diana Jeuda said that motivating Labour Party activists to volunteer in election campaigns was not about the structures, but about finding the people who wanted to work. She added that Party members should feel confident about selling the government's achievements because, according to her, there were suitcases full of achievements. The GMB – Steve Pickering and Mary Turner – spoke against the list and multi-member constituency system for European elections.

Ian McCartney MP, one of the three representatives appointed to the NEC by the cabinet, supported Millbank's analysis in a very gung-ho way. He said that the letters he had received from Party activists fell into two camps: those who worked and those who didn't. He denied that the ones who didn't work had refused to do so because of discontent with government policies, but he offered no other explanation. He was firmly in favour of restructuring local parties. McDonagh came back and said this was not about blaming activists. But the whole tenor of her remarks, and of the Millbank paper, was to that effect – it was Labour Party members and activists who had failed to work, and had thereby let the government down. The paper was passed with only the Grassroots Alliance and the GMB voting against.

Blair had left before the discussion on elections was taken, but in his report he had referred to the need "to revitalise our own organisation", whilst also saying that the idea that there had been insufficient campaigning for the European elections was "nonsense". The trade unions were anxious to make up some ground after the bad publicity that they had received over the National Policy Forum. Anne Picking of UNISON insisted that, "contrary to the report in *Tribune*, the trade unions are not putty in the hands of the government", and then thanked Blair for the government's concession at the National Policy Forum on the job security of non-clinical NHS staff in Private Finance Initiative transfers. "Our position on PFI has not changed, but we welcome the opportunity." Mary Turner of the GMB echoed her thanks. Blair replied, "We want to protect the workforce, but PFI is still the right way to go."

I asked Blair about the proposals in the Asylum Bill to restrict asylum seekers' ability to bring judicial reviews against Home Office decisions, and the fact that the campaigning organisation JUSTICE had condemned the Bill as contrary to human rights. I also asked if the Labour Party would voluntarily implement a recommendation of the Neill Committee that the specific amount of donations or sponsorships in excess of £5,000 should be disclosed, along with the names of donors and sponsors. I noted that the recommendation of the Neill Committee was already contained in a Bill on the funding of political parties and that therefore the Party would be required to make such disclosures in the future in any case. Why not do it now, voluntarily? As I spoke, Blair seemed to make a point of ignoring me and talking to Margaret Beckett, sitting next to him. When he did respond to my comments, he said he would not reconsider the Asylum Bill, and claimed that the asylum system was "fraudulent and corrupt". He also saw no need to move beyond our present position on disclosure of Party donations – until we were required to do so by law.

The rest of the meeting was taken up with more mundane Party business. The NEC was asked to approve rule changes to be put to Annual Conference. Slipped in amongst eleven rule changes was a proposal to elect the constituency representative on the National Constitutional Committee by conference delegates rather than as part of the NEC one member, one vote ballot, as in the past. There was only one reason for the change in elector-ate: the one member, one vote ballot had returned Grassroots Alliance candidates for the previous two years and Millbank calculated that conference delegates are more malleable, easier to canvass by Millbank (since they are all in one place) and therefore more likely to return the favoured candidate. Pete

Willsman (still a member of the NEC until October) said in no uncertain terms that that was the hidden agenda.

I seized the opportunity to propose three additional rule changes for the NEC to put before Conference: to prevent members of the House of Lords standing in the CLP section of the NEC (the "Sawyer" amendment), to declare a vacancy in the CLP section if a member is elected either to Parliament or to the European Parliament (the "Cashman" amendment), and to establish fixed dates for NEC elections, so that they could not be moved around the calendar at Millbank's whim. McDonagh's response was that rule changes were "serious business" and that amendments with additional rule changes could not be tabled "just like that". Margaret Prosser said that NEC members should not bring amendments straight to the NEC, but that these proposals should go to the Organisation Sub-committee (which was next scheduled to meet in November, after Conference). The Chair ruled my amendments out of order for that reason and no vote was taken. Millbank's rule changes were proposed and voted on *en bloc*. The only opposition was from the three Grassroots Alliance representatives present.

We then moved on to guidelines for the National Policy Forum, and I proposed some amendments to those guidelines. This time, my amendments were ruled out of order on the grounds that the guidelines were out for consultation. The carve-up was becoming so embarrassingly obvious that Diana Jeuda objected, and said that I should be allowed to propose my amendments. However, the Chair insisted that the amendments were out of order, refused to take a vote, and we moved on. A week later, the *Independent* revealed the real agenda behind the proposal to "reform and modernise" local parties under the headline: "Blair to strip last power of left wing".

The next meeting of the NEC, held on 21 September 1999, was extraordinary in several respects. At first, it appeared to be business as usual. The only advance hint of anything unexpected was an obscurely titled item on the agenda: "Westminster re-selections: application for dual mandate". No paper was attached and we wondered what it referred to.

Three weeks earlier, the news had been dominated by East Timor. After twenty-five years of resistance to Indonesian repression, at a cost of the lives of one third of the local people, East Timor had voted for independence. Tragically, that vote had been overseen by the Indonesian government, not by the UN, although there were UN observers. After over 90 per cent of the electorate had braved intimidation to cast their ballots for independence, armed groups, called "local militias" but equipped and assisted by the Indonesian military, embarked on an indiscriminate slaughter throughout the country. The complicity of all those countries that had sold arms to the Indonesian military was evident. I went into the NEC furious at the government's willingness to sell arms to murderers, and (more parochially) mindful that the Indonesian ambassador was still to be a guest at Conference, to be held the following week.

Blair told us that Conference would be an opportunity to get across the big picture. "We are combining modernisation with social justice. . . . We must be highly disciplined, united, forward-looking, committed to social justice and a unified and competent Party of government. . . . We need to get across what the government has achieved – to our own supporters as much as to anyone else." He was anxious to stress public services, an anxiety that sat rather uneasily with his reported comments to the British Venture Capitalist Association in July that public sector workers were resistant to change, and dealing with them had left him with "scars on my back". He was challenged directly by Mary Turner of the GMB, who said, "Your speech attacking public sector workers was not helpful. You should praise rather than attack." His response was: "I never actually talked about public service workers – these things get in and out of the papers. . . . I didn't attack public service workers – I was talking about reforming public services."

I asked Blair how the continuation of arms sales to Indonesia since 1997 could be justified under an "ethical foreign policy", and would he now support withdrawing the invitation to the Indonesian ambassador? He replied that arms sales were not the issue and claimed that the killings in East Timor had been carried

out by the local militias, not by the Indonesian military – a claim
later discredited by the UN. After a hurried consultation with
Margaret McDonagh, he said that the Indonesian ambassador
would not be coming to Conference. McDonagh later added that
the invitation had already been withdrawn. The subsequent minutes, however, referred to the "ambassador for East Timor" not
being invited to the Conference, suggesting that Millbank had
still not exactly grasped the point.

Blair concluded with his usual warning about the dire consequences of dissent. "If you look at the 1960s, 1970s and 1980s, the
Labour Party must never again lose the competence or capacity
to govern because of internal differences. We are stronger today.
It's been a painful and difficult process. If we forget how we got
here, we will be back to where we started. In the 1970s, the PLP
and the Labour Party lost touch with each other – that must never
happen again."

Blair left, and we took the report from the European Parliament Labour Group. As Alan Donnelly was speaking, there was
suddenly an interruption from Ian McCartney (who had earlier
left the room to take a phone call). He was shaking, and said that
he had just been informed that his son had been found dead.
There was a collective gasp. John Prescott and various Millbank
officials went over to McCartney and took him out of the room.
The Chair said that we should adjourn for five minutes. Unusually
for a political meeting, there was not an immediate rush towards
the tea and coffee. People were sitting round the table, silent and
shocked. The sudden intrusion of this terrible personal tragedy
made the routine deliberations of the meeting seem even more
unreal than usual.

The adjournment lasted about twenty minutes and, towards the
end of it, members were back to discussing politics over coffee.
Derek Hodgson (a trade union representative on the NEC, and
General Secretary of the CWU) was manoeuvring to ensure that
the CWU motion opposing privatisation of the Post Office would
be debated at Conference. This would require Conference to
debate five, rather than four, contemporary motions, as in the
past. (Contemporary motions – that is, motions restricted to

events that have arisen since the National Policy Forum last met in July – are the only type of motions allowable at the modernised Labour Party Conference.) If only four were taken, for reasons that I never fully understood, everyone agreed that it was unlikely that privatisation of the Post Office would be amongst them. Pete Willsman, ever the authority on Conference procedure, assured Hodgson that there were no rules requiring the restriction of contemporary motions to four rather than five.

When we resumed, we came to the item on "application for dual mandate". A confidential report was handed round. Each copy was numbered and was to be returned. In essence, Ron Davies (who had resigned as Leader of the Welsh Party and Secretary of State for Wales after his "moment of madness" on Clapham Common a year earlier) wished to put his name forward to be reselected for his Westminster seat, whilst remaining a member of the Welsh Assembly. Labour Party rules forbid the exercise of such a "dual mandate". MPs cannot also be MEPs, or members of the Scottish Parliament or Welsh Assembly. The NEC has authority to override that rule in exceptional circumstances, and Davies wanted to be considered as an exceptional circumstance.

Margaret McDonagh described the rule against a dual mandate as a "puritanical view". She said that she would prefer that the issue was not debated, just voted on, although she would answer questions. Uniquely for a Millbank document, the report handed round did not contain any recommendations, and McDonagh made a point of not making a recommendation one way or another. The decision was left up to the NEC. Millbank had no line on it, and so the debate was not the usual contest between Millbank loyalists and the Grassroots Alliance. For once, the decision had not been made in advance.

The combination of sympathy for Ron Davies and his particular misfortunes, together with the shock still overhanging the meeting as a result of McCartney's tragedy, resulted in a discussion that was humane, good-tempered and genuinely open. Members of the NEC made it clear that they did want a discussion, and McDonagh and the Chair did not move to prevent it. There was a consensus in principle against dual mandates, despite Mc-Donagh's view. Alan Donnelly spoke about how the rule prohibiting dual mandates had come about after some MEPs had used their offices and political resources to campaign for selection in Westminster seats. There was general anxiety, best expressed by Dianne Hayter, at the message that would be sent to the Welsh electorate if such a prominent member of the Welsh Assembly was seen to treat it with less importance than he treated Westminster. If the NEC voted against a dual mandate, Davies would still have a choice: either to remain in the Welsh Assembly, or to resign from the Assembly and seek reselection as a Westminster MP. The decision was eventually made to refuse Davies's application, by a vote of twenty-one to three (the three being Maggie Jones, Anne Picking and Pete Willsman). That afternoon, having received the NEC's decision, Davies announced that he would not stand again for Westminster, but would remain in the Welsh Assembly.

The spirit of unity and humanity did not last long. Towards the end of the meeting, we came to the item on arrangements for Party Conference. Derek Hodgson asked McDonagh how many contemporary resolutions would be taken. She replied that the rule was four. Hodgson, relying on Pete's earlier assurances over coffee, challenged her assertion that it was a rule. I had my copy of the rule book open. The rules are silent as to how many contemporary motions can be taken and I passed the rule book to Hodgson. McDonagh's response was to insist: "It is a rule, but it is not written down." Hodgson fumed, and in the end he got his five contemporary motions. As it turned out, he didn't need them since privatisation of the Post Office topped the priorities ballot for contemporary motions.

Conference the following week was the most stage-managed yet. We had been told at the NEC that certain slogans would be emphasised: "for the many, not the few", "future not past", "toward the 21st century". By the end of conference week, many delegates and journalists were sick of hearing these phrases repeated. If delegates wanted to speak at Conference, they had to introduce themselves to the "delegate support office", which would discuss with them what they intended to say. If a delegate wanted to disagree with government policy, they would be politely thanked, and told that their name would be passed to the Chair. Those delegates then tried very hard to get into the debate, waving their conference papers and trying to attract the Chair's eye, but were rarely successful. Other delegates, who had given the right answers to the delegate support office, were ushered into a small room with a speechwriter and a word-processor and given "speakers' notes" to assist them. Delegate after delegate came to the rostrum and declared that the government was acting "for the many, not the few". Seconds into a speech, these mantras would make it obvious if a delegate had received the assistance of Millbank's speechwriters. Mark, Pete and I, sitting up at the front of the assembly, started playing a game: how quickly could we spot the platform plant?

The conference was celebrating the Labour Party's centenary. A video on the Party's history was shown during Conference session and there were various brochures. The general thrust of both video and brochures was that the Party was set up, a long time ago, by men in cloth caps. Their motivation was understandable for their age, but now the Party had moved on and "modernised". The old values were no longer appropriate. Neil Kinnock had been "a great Leader" but Jim Callaghan was considered too "Old Labour" and hardly got a mention.

Sitting up at the front of Conference was a strange experience, given that I had been placed behind a pillar the previous year. There were two tables for the NEC. Favoured members would sit up on the platform, with the Chair, McDonagh, Blair and cabinet ministers. Lower down, but still at the front facing Conference, was a table for less-exalted NEC members. Mark, Pete and I staked our claim to three seats on the lower table. Pete and I were never honoured with an invitation to sit on the main platform, but during a poorly attended session of Conference, when some embarrassing gaps appeared on the platform, Mark was invited to make up the numbers. Ten minutes later, he was back with Pete and me. He had clapped the wrong speaker and been asked to leave.

There was no longer anything at Party Conference that could be fairly described as a "debate". Proceedings were organised around the nine policy documents, but since these could not be amended, the discussion was aimless. During the session dedicated to each policy document, the relevant cabinet minister got to make a "keynote speech". Not surprisingly, given the pointlessness of the proceedings, the hall filled up only when the big names – Gordon Brown, John Prescott, Robin Cook – took their turn with the rostrum and autocue. Along with the government ministers and their uncritical supporters among the delegates, some other speakers seemed to be favoured for no discernible reason. For example, one Party member (not a delegate) was brought onto the platform to praise New Labour's promotion of businesses, and took the opportunity to plug his own computer company as he did so. Two ambitious Blairites from the 1997 parliamentary intake, Yvette Cooper and Stephen Twigg, were standing as Millbank's candidates against Audrey Wise MP for Conference Arrangements Committee (which is elected by Conference delegates) and were given the opportunity to address Conference before the ballot was held. Wise and her fellow Grassroots Alliance candidate for the committee, George McManus, were not given the same opportunity. At the beginning and end of Conference sessions there would be amusing videos or inspirational music. Frequently, the amusing videos featured Tony Robinson ("Baldrick" in *Blackadder*), coincidentally rumoured to be standing for the NEC to replace Cashman the following year.

Most of the real business went on outside the hall. There were around 18,000 exhibitors, businesspeople or lobbyists as against around 1,800 delegates. Those people are not there for conference discussions. Outside the main hall, the exhibition area, the cafés and the bars were buzzing. I recognised a lot of familiar faces from Labour parties around the country – not delegates, but upwardly mobile New Labourites hoping to network and obtain some useful contacts. The combination of the dreary goings-on inside the hall and the gossip and interchange outside the hall meant that coffee bars were always fuller than the conference chamber.

In the evenings, some delegates would still attend the traditional fringe meetings, but they were becoming visibly fewer
with each passing year. Instead, unions and corporations sponsored receptions, and cabinet ministers and other dignitaries
made the rounds of these receptions. There are, in effect, two
conferences. The first is attended by delegates who still want to
discuss politics; they follow the discussion, read leaflets and
documents, discuss the machinations that go on behind the
scenes, and they care about the outcome of the whole thing. The
second is attended by other delegates, along with a large number
of hangers-on, networkers, lobbyists, and corporate agents. They
have little interest in Conference, save for providing an appreci-
ative audience for the "keynote speeches", but a lot of interest in
networking. The trade unions try to maintain an uneasy balance
between the two conferences. Cabinet ministers overwhelmingly
favour the second and, save for their keynote speeches, pay little
attention to the first.

At the 1999 Party Conference, the consultation on "The 21st
Century Party" document was launched. In the end, this proved
to be one of the few consultation exercises that did not quite
go Millbank's way. According to Millbank, the reason Party
members did not turn out in recent election campaigns was
because they were bogged down in internal bureaucracy. It was
time to get rid of the endless, tedious, pointless meetings, and
thereby liberate Party members to spring into campaigning activity. The political agenda here was clear-cut. The endless, tedious,
pointless meetings that Millbank wants to abolish are principally
constituency parties' general committees – the last redoubts of
democratic practice in the Labour Party. Some of Millbank's
claims about these meetings are true: too often they are rife with
jargon, unwelcoming to new members, and bogged down in
administrative detail. But it is also true that these meetings are
where Party members come together to discuss politics – and
Labour Party members enjoy a good political discussion. They
also enjoy the chance to have an effect on policy – and constituency general committee meetings accept motions and take votes.
If the constituency is represented by a Labour MP, the general

committee meeting is the only forum where that MP can be questioned and held to account by the Party members who got him or her elected. A number of New Labour MPs had been given a very hard time when they voted to cut lone parent benefit, and Millbank wanted to spare them such ordeals in the future. The purpose of the 21st Century Party consultation was to cajole the Party into abolishing the "boring" general committees and replacing them with small local executives (who would report to nobody) and the occasional powerless all-member discussion meeting. Above all, the push was to get rid of that lingering hangover from Old Labour, the tendency to take votes on political issues. The document was sent to local parties for consultation. The results of the consultation were reported to the NEC in July 2000, and it was clear then that Millbank had not succeeded in convincing local parties to abolish their decision-making structures.

There were two moments when Conference regained its old fire. On the Monday afternoon, during the session on the economic policy document (for consultation only – no decisions were to be made until the following year), Barbara Castle was given a chance to speak on pensions. The Chair, Vernon Hince, foolishly interrupted her to say that she had overrun her time. Delegates shouted, "Let Barbara finish," and Hince ended up allowing her to take as long as she wanted. People were hanging on Castle's every word. Millbank apparatchiks rushed around looking anxious, even though there was to be no vote on the contentious issue, unless some brave delegate stepped forward to oppose the economic policy document as a whole. Claire Wadey, a delegate from Brighton and a Campaign for Labour Party Democracy activist, had the nerve to do just that. She explained clearly that she regretted being put in this position, but her constituency party was against Private Finance Initiative schemes and unless the support for them was removed from the document, she would have to vote against it as a whole. Conference, its nerve bolstered by Castle's speech, clapped her enthusiastically. From the chair, Hince reminded delegates that there was no opportunity for Conference to refer back part of the document. He then put the whole of the document to a vote – and, to general amazement, Conference voted against it. So many delegates were furious at not being allowed a specific vote on PFI or pensions that they were prepared, for once, not to do as they were told.

Sitting at the front, Mark, Pete and I could see that the vote was clearly lost. Hince became agitated and called for a revote – on the grounds that delegates must have not understood the purpose of the first vote. So there was a second vote – and the document was again defeated. Suddenly, Conference was growling. At that night's fringe meetings, Claire Wadey was the heroine of the left.

The next morning, Michael Cashman was chairing Conference. His very first announcement was that Conference had been "confused" the previous afternoon and he was going to take another vote on the economic policy document. Claire Wadey was standing up at the front of Conference waving her order paper. Cashman's script had clearly anticipated that she would move reference back of his announcement that the vote would be taken again. Like the actor he is, Cashman ploughed on with his script and announced that those in favour of the reference back (not yet actually moved by anyone) should vote against the report from Conference Arrangements Committee (which recommended that the vote should be taken again). He had jumped the gun. Claire managed to get to the rostrum, and politely informed Cashman that she had not yet moved the reference back, but would do so now. She expressed regret that events had got so out of hand, but she was mandated by her constituency to vote against PFI and could not therefore support the economic policy document. Millbank officials managed to spin the press coverage so that Claire's regret was reported, but not her determination to force the issue. Conference then went to a vote, and, of course, enough arms had been twisted the previous evening so that this time the vote went according to the Millbank script. The economic policy document was approved.

We were all anticipating another old-fashioned row over the CWU motion opposing privatisation of the Post Office. A year earlier, Derek Hodgson had been the only voice of passion at the

1998 conference when he had spoken against privatisation. Of the five contemporary motions admitted for debate, the two contentious ones were on privatisation of the Post Office and the Working Time Directive (the directive limits the working week to 48 hours; the government was proposing to allow some employers to opt out and require their employees to work longer hours). The NEC was scheduled to meet on the Tuesday morning, at 7.30am, to decide its views and recommendations on the contemporary motions. This meeting lasted only twenty minutes, and only the three noncontentious composites were put before the NEC. It appeared that no deals had yet been hammered out on either of the contentious issues, so the NEC would have to meet again the following morning.

Throughout the Monday and Tuesday of Conference, Derek Hodgson had been closeted with Stephen Byers and a Downing Street policy officer, negotiating a compromise. Even when Hodgson briefly appeared in the conference hall, the Downing Street official was constantly at his side. Delegates remained in the dark. I arrived at the NEC on Wednesday morning at 7.40am, ten minutes late, expecting a battle over the two contentious motions. As I walked in, I was told that the NEC meeting had already concluded its business. Both motions had been reworded so that they posed no threat to the leadership, and the NEC had accepted them without discussion. The condemnation of the opt-out regulations had been edited out of the composite on the Working Time Directive. Instead, it now expressed "concern" at the regulations, but welcomed assurances from the government that the regulations applied only to senior managers.

The deal on the Post Office was even more ambiguous. Hodgson had conceded that "reform is necessary if the Post Office is to adapt to the changing communications market of the next century". In return, Byers had conceded the following verbiage: "Conference believes that the Post Office should remain a 100 per cent publicly owned service and therefore, while concerned that the government plans to turn the corporation into a plc, welcomes the assurance to the House of Commons of the Secretary of State for Trade and Industry." This was followed by a firmer statement: "Conference urges that a commitment to full public ownership of the Post Office is clearly contained in the Labour Party manifesto for the next general election." But all the government itself was asked to do was to consult, to seek the views of the regulator, and to make assessments. Both sides claimed victory. Hodgson could deliver his tub-thumping speech to Conference in defence of a publicly owned Post Office. Byers could reassure big business that the motion committed him to nothing. And the NEC was delighted at having avoided a public row.

By the Friday morning, most delegates had gone home. To my surprise, the hall was still full, but Pete informed me that most of the audience were actually exhibitors from outside the main conference hall, who had been asked to come in so that the hall would appear full for the cameras. Margaret McDonagh subsequently told the NEC that they had filled up the hall with local sixth-formers and unidentified Labour Party members. I walked in to Conference to find Tom Sawyer dressed as Keir Hardie, telling jokes. Various young people were called up to tell the hall how much their lives have improved under the New Labour government. John O'Farrell, author of *Things Can Only Get Better* (a somewhat cynical account of life as a Labour Party member during the 1980s), and TV scriptwriter for *Spitting Image* and *Have I Got News For You* (amongst others), told a few jokes (funnier than Tom Sawyer's, but not much), and promoted his book and himself – he is now on the National Parliamentary Panel, looking for a parliamentary seat. Conference sang the quickest, and quietest, chorus of "The Red Flag" I have ever heard. Blair then made a triumphant exit, parading from one side of the hall to the other, surrounded by photographers, and bathed in coloured lights. This performance culminated in his disappearing behind the curtain, but as he did so sticking out a hand with a thumbs-up, framed by a spotlight.

7

The Spectre Haunting New Labour

From November 1997, when the Queen's Speech announced the creation of a directly elected mayor for London and a Greater London Assembly, the question of Ken Livingstone loomed ever larger in the collective mind of the Labour Party. Number Ten's determination to prevent him from becoming mayor was so well-publicised, and said to be so implacable, that most of us wondered not whether he would be prevented from standing as the Labour candidate, but how.

When I was first elected to the National Executive Committee in October 1998, I assumed that the NEC would shortly be presented with Millbank's plan for the selection of the Labour candidate for mayor. In the end, the uncertainty dragged on until October 1999, making Labour the last major political party to commence its selection process for the London poll. Former Tory MP and novelist Jeffrey Archer and Susan Kramer for the Liberal Democrats had already been chosen as their parties' standard-bearers before the Labour Party had even settled on a process of selection. There was never any effort to explain or justify to the NEC the perpetual delay. We all knew that Millbank was struggling both to unearth a candidate who could beat Ken Livingstone and to concoct a selection process that would give that candidate the maximum advantage. Livingstone, as the leader of the GLC until Thatcher had abolished it, was widely regarded as the choice of most London Labour Party members to run as mayor. He had been MP for Brent East since 1987, but was still "Mr London" in the eyes of most Londoners and Labour Party members.

At this point, it was widely assumed that the selection would be a one member, one vote ballot rather than the product of an electoral college, and that the main issue would be about the shortlist. In June 1998, the London Labour Party Conference called near-unanimously, with just one vote against, for the automatic inclusion on the shortlist of any candidate who had obtained at least ten constituency nominations. Livingstone, of course, would have no difficulty in collecting the ten nominations. Unfortunately, London Labour Party policy is made not by its conference but by its "board" (New Labour-speak for "executive"), and then must be approved by the NEC. The Board met on 10 November 1998 and refused to follow the policy of its own conference, recommending instead (on Millbank's advice) that there be a system of self-nomination by potential candidates, who would be interviewed by a selection panel which would then draw up the shortlist. There would be no constituency nominations and nobody could claim a right to be on the shortlist. At the London Board, there were four votes against the Millbank stitch-up: two constituency representatives (Christine Shawcroft and Paul Tyler) and two from the TGWU.

At the Board meeting, the TGWU proposed a compromise: any candidate receiving nominations from at least ten constituency parties would have the right to be on the shortlist, but others could put their names forward and be interviewed by a selection panel. This was described as the "twin-track approach", and Margaret Prosser, then running for Deputy General Secretary of the TGWU, was the front person promoting it. If that system were adopted, Livingstone could not be blocked from the shortlist. Despite support from the GPMU and UNISON, the Board voted down the compromise.

In the meantime, Millbank were pursuing their long-running campaign to discredit Livingstone. In the autumn of 1998, at least one journalist was approached by a senior member of the government with a copy of Millbank's private dossier on Livingstone. But they were having trouble finding a challenger. It appeared that Tony Banks refused the poison chalice – allegedly disappointing Millbank, who it was said saw him as some kind of more malleable Livingstone understudy. Mo Mowlam made a point of turning up at the launch of Livingstone's biography in April 1999, and of being photographed arm in arm with the man himself, thus scuppering speculation that she would emerge to take on Ken. Glenda Jackson's name had been in the frame for some months, and she launched her campaign at Conference in October 1999. Her policies, in particular her support for public–private partnership financing of the London underground, were identical to those of the government. However, despite the rumour that she was initially encouraged to stand by Downing Street, Millbank appeared to blow hot and cold on her. One minute she was being talked up as the main challenger to Livingstone; the next she was portrayed as an also-ran. Trevor Phillips was another candidate whose policies were clearly New Labour, who would cause the government no difficulty, and who appeared to have been initially encouraged to stand by Millbank. Again, he was talked up and run down (Millbank were hedging their bets). Meanwhile, New Labour kept floating more names: Richard Branson or Bob Ayling (subsequently forced to resign as chair of British Airways), Joanna Lumley or Delia Smith. Then, during Conference week, Nick Raynsford announced his candidature, apparently in all seriousness and with Millbank's blessing, only to withdraw less than two weeks later in favour of Frank Dobson, the final Millbank choice.

As Livingstone himself observed, Millbank's habit of floating names and then retreating from them was a tactical folly. None of his potential challengers was given enough time to establish themselves in the public's mind. What's more, the persistently publicised fact that Millbank was moving heaven and earth to stop him gave him more exposure and added to his populist appeal. His opposition to public–private partnership financing was endorsed by the majority of Londoners, and anyone saddled with that policy by Downing Street was going to have a hard time. In February 1999, over 1,000 people attended a "Let Ken Living-stone Stand" rally in Westminster Central Hall.

It wasn't just the mayor that Millbank was worried about. It was vital that the future Labour members of the Greater London Assembly would not rock the boat. Party members were selecting their candidates for the Greater London Assembly over the summer of 1999. Potential candidates were invited to apply to a selection panel. The panel was composed of Millbank appointees. Anybody suspected of being a Livingstone supporter was weeded out, along with anyone with any record of independence from the leadership machine. The Greater London Assembly was to consist of twenty-five members: fourteen elected on a first-past-the-post basis in single-member constituencies and eleven from top-up lists according to the parties' share of the poll. Faced with a ballot paper of the approved candidates – different faces all spouting the same New Labour shibboleths – I decided not to vote in the selection for constituency candidates. When it came to the eleven top-up seats, we weren't even given this semblance of choice. The eleven were chosen, and placed in order, by the Millbank-appointed selection panel.

Back in July, Frank Dobson had commented on the *Today* programme that he loved being Secretary of State for Health and did not want any other job. At Conference, he had been reported as expressing relief that Raynsford was entering the fray. The next week, members of the NEC were informed that the NEC would hold a special meeting on 12 October to determine the selection procedure for mayor. This date was already earmarked as another NEC away-day at Congress House. The meeting to determine the selection procedure was to be slotted in at the beginning of the away-day. The agenda itself contained no clues as to Millbank's thinking, merely announcing "agreement of procedure for selection of London mayor". No papers were sent out in advance.

This was the first meeting of the newly elected 1999–2000 NEC. Its political composition had hardly changed. The constituency places were now split: three to the Millbank slate (Sawyer, Cashman, Jeuda) and three Grassroots Alliance (Mark, Christine, myself). But we had an unexpected success in the Parliamentary Labour Party section. The MPs and MEPs, voting this time in a secret ballot, had rejected two of the three sitting Blairite representatives (Pauline Green and Anne Begg) in favour of Dennis Skinner and Helen Jackson. Skinner's result was an obvious victory for the left. Jackson, too, had stood as an independent, distancing herself from the Blairite slate, and MPs had supported her on that basis. As far as NEC votes went, that meant that the Grassroots Alliance continued to obtain a grand total of four votes out of thirty-three.

On the evening of 11 October, I spoke to Simon Fletcher, Livingstone's assistant, who told me there were rumours that an electoral college for the selection would be proposed. It appeared that the trade union representatives on the NEC had met that evening and that Margaret Prosser, Treasurer of the Party and a TGWU official, had informed them that there would be an electoral college. It was obvious why Millbank would prefer this device. Despite the bad publicity and resentment amongst Party members in Wales, the Welsh leadership election experience had confirmed that Millbank's influence over the trade union and MPs' and candidates' sections of the electoral college could virtually guarantee a Millbank win. The mayor for London was a wholly new position – the first directly elected mayor in Britain – and Millbank therefore had a blank slate on which to impose whatever selection procedure it chose. However, to do so it would have to face down the previous promises that the selection would be by one member, one vote. Indeed, in May 1999, Nick Raynsford, as Minister for London, had assured the Commons that the selection would be conducted in this manner.

We arrived at Congress House to be confronted with four dense documents: the principles governing the selection, the procedural rules, a statement of "candidate qualities" and a code of conduct governing the selection. Vernon Hince, now Chair of the Party, asked if members wanted time to read them before the discussion started, but there were cries around the table of "No, let's just agree it now." The documents recommended that the shortlist be drawn up by a selection panel, thus ignoring the view of the London Labour Party Conference and the "twin-track" compromise proposed by the TGWU. It seemed that Livingstone's fate would be determined by the selection panel.

The papers recommended selection by an electoral college comprised of one third London Labour Party members, one third trade unions and one third London MPs, MEPs and GLA candidates. Each vote cast by a London MP, MEP or GLA candidate would thus be worth the combined votes of 1,000 ordinary Party members. It was clear that the more reliable members of the NEC had been lined up to attack any criticism voiced by the Grassroots Alliance. Blair and Prescott were not present; they didn't need to be – the votes were guaranteed. McDonagh kicked the discussion off by claiming that an electoral college was fair because "that's what we've always done". This was not precisely true. For the election for London mayor, Millbank did not impose on the unions the same requirement made of them under the rules for electing the Leader and Deputy Leader of the Party – to ballot their own members before casting their block vote. Nor was the "payroll section" of the college the same. For the election of Leader and Deputy Leader, one third of the college is made up by the Parliamentary Labour Party, as agreed at the historic Wembley conference in 1981 – a major advance in Party democracy, since previously the PLP alone chose the Leader. The disproportionate vote wielded by the PLP in electing the Party Leader is on the whole accepted by Party members. After all, the Leader of the Party becomes Prime Minister when Labour has a majority in the House of Commons, and clearly must have substantial support of the PLP in order to function effectively. However, in the London mayoral electoral college, the principles determining who would be eligible in the "payroll" section were arbitrary. Why should London MEPs have a block vote worth 1,000 votes each in the selection for the London mayor? Why did London MPs enjoy such disproportionate influence, when the mayor would be working not with them but with the GLA members?

Christine Shawcroft, at her first NEC meeting, spoke immediately after Margaret McDonagh and argued for the London Labour Party Conference position – that a candidate receiving ten nominations should have a right to be on the shortlist. She warned that the Party in London should avoid the kind of bad publicity and electoral consequences that had resulted from the carve-up in Wales. Margaret Prosser replied directly to Christine, defending the formula of self-nomination plus a final decision by the selection board. This was wholly inconsistent with her position a year previously, when she had publicly argued for the twin-track approach. In between, Prosser had succeeded in her campaign to become TGWU Deputy General Secretary. The *Independent* reported the following day that it was Prosser who first suggested to Millbank officials the idea of an electoral college as a mechanism to prevent Livingstone's selection. Clive Soley came up with his usual defence of selection panels: "people who appear in front of them say it's a fairer system".

As the discussion went on, the Grassroots Alliance was accused of wanting to prevent trade union participation in the selection of a candidate and of special pleading for London. We were accused of wanting to exclude women and ethnic minorities who (according to the Millbank mantra) are more likely to succeed through selection panels than through a constituency nomination process. (This claim directly ignores the disproportionate rejection of black candidates by the selection panel for the GLA.) Much was made of the fact that the left had opposed John Smith's original proposals for one member, one vote. The reality is that both sides have done a volte-face, with the left championing one member, one vote, and New Labour now determined to dilute or abolish all exercises of the individual franchise within the Party. Speaking only for myself, I readily admit that the left's opposition to one member, one vote in the late 1980s and early 1990s, which I shared at the time, was a mistake.

I asked about the timetable for the selection. McDonagh accused me of wanting to interfere with the autonomy of the London Labour Party; the London Board should set the timetable, she said. She went on to argue that any procedure other than self-nomination through a selection panel would take more than three months and was therefore unacceptably long. (Six weeks later, the NEC agreed a timetable for the selection that ran to mid-February 2000 – a period of more than five months.) We moved on to the specifics. Millbank had declared that candidates were not to have access to membership lists. Helen Jackson, Diana Jeuda, Mark Seddon, Margaret Prosser and I all objected to this, on the grounds that certain favoured candidates were bound to obtain membership lists, and that making lists available to all candidates would create a level playing field. McDonagh compromised by agreeing that all shortlisted candidates would have the opportunity to circulate two statements to all London Party members – upon payment of postage and administrative expenses. She admitted that in her original opposition to circulating material, "My control-freakery got the better of me." Access to membership lists turned out to be a key issue during the selection – Dobson used the membership lists given him by party officials to bombard members with campaign materials, not least personal attacks on Livingstone – and the concession of two official mailings sent round by Party officials became meaningless given Dobson's specific access.

At the NEC, Christine asked if we could vote separately on the four papers relating to the London selection so that NEC members who had indicated discontent with some of the procedural detail could have a chance to express it. Vernon Hince refused. The papers were passed in one vote, by twenty-one votes to four (Christine, Mark, Dennis Skinner, and me). There was one more apparently formal piece of business to deal with: membership of NEC sub-committees. I remained on the Local Government Sub-committee, but Christine was kept off everything. She protested, and I proposed her for membership of the Party Development Sub-committee. The four of us voted for her to join the Party Development Sub-committee. Everyone else voted against.

The meeting then turned into the NEC away-day. Christine and Dennis left. Mark and I remained for a short while, but left in horror as we were informed, by Hazel Blears MP, that having got "New Labour", we were now embarking on "new democracy". Whilst the NEC pursued its away-day ruminations, London and South-East trade unionists were meeting in another room in Congress House. They had been informed – even before the vote had been taken at the NEC – that it had been decided that there would be an electoral college for the selection of Labour candidate for London mayor. Simultaneously, Dobson announced his campaign to be the Labour mayoral candidate, supported by Tony Banks and Nick Raynsford. Suddenly, candidates were dropping like flies. Dobson was clearly Millbank's preference. Trevor Phillips withdrew a few days later – and was rewarded a few weeks later with the number one position on the Labour top-up list for the Greater London Assembly, which meant he was assured of a seat. Glenda Jackson was rumoured to be withdrawing, but to her credit stayed in the race.

That evening on *Newsnight*, all four Labour candidates for mayor (Livingstone, Jackson, Dobson, Phillips – shortly to withdraw) expressed surprise at the imposition of an electoral college. All said that they had expected the selection to be by one member, one vote. The *Independent* the following day was pretty explicit as to the purpose of the electoral college, quoting a Millbank insider: "We want to see Ken's blood on the carpet. This is the way to do it."

Finally, after months of shadow-boxing, at least there was the possibility of a real contest (although if Ken were to be excluded from the shortlist by the selection panel, not much of one). Within days of the NEC meeting, London Labour Party members were deluged with leaflets from the Dobson camp. The material was glossy, with endorsements from London MPs and council leaders (but not from ordinary Party members). Within two weeks, I had received three mailshots from Dobson. In November, the campaign heated up. Tony Blair found the time to appear at several large meetings with Party members in London. Billed as "question and answer" sessions with the Prime Minister, open to Party members (and also the press), paid for with Party funds, the sessions were in fact devoted to promoting Dobson and attacking Livingstone (whom Blair euphemistically referred to as "another candidate"). Neil Kinnock joined Blair on one platform – you'd have thought that by now someone would realise this man is not a vote winner, even among Party members.

Dobson's campaign took a more and more personal slant. He accused Livingstone of being backed by the Tories, Liberals and the far left. There was a constant refrain (promoted by Blair) that the Party could not risk a return to the early 1980s. Livingstone was called "chameleon Ken". At the same time, various London MPs authored newspaper pieces in which they claimed that they had worked with Ken in the London Labour Party in the 1980s and knew from personal experience that he could not be trusted. Bizarrely, Livingstone was accused of losing the 1987 general election (despite the fact that the Labour vote in London increased in 1987). The most absurd intervention came from Michael Cashman, who claimed that Livingstone, by supporting lesbian and gay rights in the 1980s, had been responsible for the Tories' introduction of the homophobic Section 28, which banned the "promotion" of homosexuality in schools.

Party members complained that Dobson's attacks flouted the code of conduct for internal party elections, which stipulated: "candidates or their agents shall not use the media to attack or denigrate other candidates in the elections". Members asked where Dobson had obtained their addresses from. They also wondered whether Dobson had not already exceeded the NEC-approved limit on campaign expenditure of £1 per London Party member – roughly £62,000.

The selection panel met at Millbank on 16 November, the day I attended my long-awaited meeting with Keith Ewing's "review" on Party finances. There was a howling gale outside, and the media had a long, uncomfortable wait. That evening, all three Labour candidates were due to address a meeting called by the RMT on the funding of the London underground. When I arrived at the Friends' Meeting House, the hall was packed with over three hundred people in the audience – tube workers and London Party members. Livingstone and Jackson were on the platform. Dobson was nowhere to be seen and had apparently not sent apologies. Nobody knew what the decision of the selection board was. Livingstone's support for refinancing the tube through a bond issue went down well, but Jackson also managed to endear herself to the audience, despite the clear lack of support for her position on the tube. She defended public–private partnership financing with gusto and guts, though she must have known there would be few takers in this crowd. By her insistence on staying in the race, despite Millbank pressure, she had shown some welcome independence of spirit.

About halfway through the meeting, Livingstone was handed a

note and left the hall to be interviewed by the press. The press told him the news that the selection board had adjourned their decision and decided to invite him for a further interview two days later. Later that evening, Livingstone, Jackson and Clive Soley (chair of the selection board) were interviewed on *Newsnight*. Paxman introduced the item by saying that all the senior political correspondents had been invited to Downing Street that evening at 5.30pm, presumably for Blair to comment on the selection board's decision, that they had waited for three hours and then all been sent away at 8.30pm. Paxman was miffed, but Jackson was incandescent. Ken later described her as being "the angriest" he had ever seen her – and the two of them by then had clashed at scores of debates. She described the decision of the selection board as "a sad day for the Party". When Paxman asked her if she was breaking the Party's code of conduct by attacking the process, her reply was "So be it!"

Soley put up a poor performance, unable to explain why the selection panel had not come to a decision. The press at the time were told by Millbank that Blair himself had decided a few days earlier that Livingstone should be on the shortlist, if only in order to prevent him looking like a martyr, but that when it came to the interview, Livingstone was so intransigent in his attitude to the Labour manifesto that the members of the selection panel (despite their instructions from Downing Street) felt that his answers were unacceptable. This line has been repeated by Andrew Rawnsley, who claims authoritative and private sources. At the time, it seemed to me as though the opposite was the case: that the panel were under instructions from Downing Street to exclude Ken, but were unable to find anything in his answers to justify exclusion. They decided to give themselves some more time and to require Livingstone to appear before them again in the vain hope of finding a hook on which to hang him, and then to consult Downing Street before they made a final decision. Of course, I accept that Rawnsley is probably better informed on Party decision making than a member of the Party's NEC.

That evening, it looked pretty clear that Ken would be excluded. Although Ken was not saying a word, it also looked pretty clear that if he was excluded, he would run as an independent. Two days later, the selection panel met and announced that, after all, Ken would be admitted onto the shortlist. Downing Street had decided that the risk of excluding him – and thus strengthening any independent candidacy he might launch – was too great. That same day Downing Street announced that Cherie was pregnant.

The NEC met five days later, on 23 November. Formally, there was only one item on the agenda dealing with the mayoral selection, headed "update on selection of Labour candidate for London Mayor/timetable". The paper was not, of course, sent out in advance. Despite there being several other long discussions on the agenda, the issue of the mayoral selection dominated the meeting. I arrived a few minutes late, as the tubes were in chaos. As I walked in, Diana Jeuda was challenging the minutes of the 12 October meeting. According to the minutes, the NEC had agreed that shortlisted candidates could send up to two mailings to each member using the Labour Party's mailing service. Jeuda's point was that the NEC gave that indication, but did not come to an actual decision. Vernon Hince put the accuracy of the minutes to a vote. Sixteen people voted to accept the minutes as they stood; four of us (Christine, Mark, Diana and I) abstained. I noted that the minutes failed to record my proposal that Christine be a member of the Party Development Sub-committee, which had been voted down, but since accuracy of the minutes seemed to be yet another issue on which the NEC divides on factional lines, I decided that it was not worth bothering with an attempted correction.

Blair spoke mainly about the upcoming Queen's Speech. His message for the day was "people think nothing's happening, but the programme is moving forward". He said that all over Europe governments were trying to reach "a new political consensus" and were embarking on "a painful process of change". He ended with the usual insistence that any criticism of the government would bring the Tories back. He briefly mentioned the mayoral selection: "it's an important decision – we've got to get it right. We've got the right policies for London. We don't want the Labour

Party to slip backwards to the early 1980s. The mess that the Tories are in is because they failed to exercise leadership."

Christine was the first to question Blair and she tackled the Livingstone issue straight off. Referring to the code of conduct on the selection of the mayor, she said that Blair's own high-profile attacks on Livingstone were contrary to the guidelines. I took the opportunity to ask Blair to reconsider the proposal to abolish the right of defendants to choose trial by jury. Mark asked whether there was any scope for the government to intervene to save the Ellington colliery, which was subject to a hostile bid. Michael Cashman responded to Christine, and sticking to the Blairite habit of never referring to Livingstone by name, said "I've spoken out against a particular candidate. I'm sick and tired of lesbian and gay rights being seen as the dustbin of good politics. Now we've moved, but we've taken thirteen years to get there. I will continue to be a pain in the side to anyone who is in opposition to me." What exactly he meant, I don't know.

The TGWU asked Blair to reconsider the proposed mechanism for allowing parents to take parental leave: the government's proposals required that parents would have to take entire weeks off, rather than just odd days, and the TGWU was concernedp that parents whose children were ill for just one or two days would be reluctant to exercise their right to time off. Mary Turner of the GMB asked about Remploy, a government-run company employing people with disabilities, which had announced closures that would result in the loss of over 1,000 jobs. Derek Hodgson wanted to be assured (again) that the Post Office would remain in public ownership. Blair responded by repeating his message that New Labour is better than the Tories. He promised to keep parental leave under review, agreed that the government would facilitate a miners' buy-out of Ellington colliery if that was what was proposed by the miners, but stated unequivocally that "no money" would be available. He said that the "difficulty with Remploy" was "money". He disagreed with me over trial by jury, saying that the right to choose trial by jury "is expensive, ineffi-cient and is being abused. The change is necessary in order to beat crime." He compared it to drug-testing – saying both were necessary to beat crime – and added, "We have to be prepared to take people on."

He then embarked on a ten-minute diatribe on the question of Ken Livingstone: "I'm not denigrating Ken Livingstone. I'm concerned at the possibility of his candidature. It depends on your view of the Labour Party in the last twenty years. In the early 1980s, Ken Livingstone was in charge [*sic*] and we had the worst election defeat. In 1997 we had the best election result. It's nothing to do with a personal attack. I refused to do that. I'm genuinely worried about the political situation in the Labour Party. All Labour governments have been torn apart by internal divisions over one group of people saying betrayal. We're told it's a different situation today, but not unless we make it different. Ken Livingstone is on the selection list. He has the right to make his case. My right is to say that there's an issue here. It would be bad for the Labour Party to go down that path. Why are so many people who are hostile to the Labour Party desperate for Livingstone to succeed? I could have kept absolutely quiet. I was in the London Labour Party in the early 1980s. It was terrible. We drove out decent people to the SDP or the Tories. If I'm exaggerating, the selection campaign will show that up. Debates should be on policy. We're not privatising but reconstructing the tube through PPP. Look at the Jubilee Line. Law and order and business development are what matters. Whoever is the Labour Party candidate, we want them to stand on good policies. We do not want to re-create a factional split . . ."

The NEC sat in silence. Blair went on and on. Most of us there had never seen him so agitated. Mark interrupted Blair to ask: "What happens if Livingstone wins?" Blair responded: "Sometimes you have to challenge conventional thinking. Why is the Tory press desperate for this to happen? The right policy is what matters. I've not said that a person must not be a candidate. The issue is has he changed or not? If someone wants to use it as a political platform or factionally within the Labour Party, it will be a disaster for the general election. There's a contrast there with the Tories who showed that if you give someone their way, it comes back and bites you." Blair appeared to be referring to

Archer, who had by this time withdrawn from the race after evidence had emerged that he had asked a friend to provide him with a false alibi to use in his 1987 libel case against the *Sun* newspaper. Mark interrupted again: "But Archer is a crook." Blair said, "This is not about personality but about policy. Has he changed? If not, it will be bad for London and bad for the Labour Party. I'm the leader. If I don't raise this, it would be wrong."

Prescott backed up Blair, saying that although he himself was not a Londoner, he had been dragged into the debate because he was carrying out the policy of the manifesto on the tube. "If Ken Livingstone challenges me, I'll have the debate." Prescott was rather more coherent than Blair. His line was that public–private partnership was in the Labour Party manifesto for the 1997 general election and therefore we were all required to implement it. This is something of an exaggeration. The 1997 manifesto read: "Labour plans a new public–private partnership to improve the Underground, safeguard its commitment to public interest and guarantee value for money to taxpayers and passengers." Livingstone argued that the wording did not require the London underground to be privately financed if the money could be cheaply and efficiently raised by other means.

As the NEC sat in slightly amazed silence, Soley chipped in: "This is one of the reasons why the commitment by the candidates to support the manifesto was so important." Blair and Prescott got up to leave (although Prescott later returned). The rest of the NEC was not nearly so exciting, although there were some minor contretemps. The main discussion was over a paper headed, "Labour in local government, problem or opportunity?" The local government representatives on the NEC – Sally Powell and Jeremy Beecham – were fuming: they had not been consulted over the content of the paper and they warned that the heading would be resented by Labour councillors. The paper was written by Millbank's Local Government Unit and its line was in keeping with Millbank's attempt to scapegoat Labour councillors for poor election results. The report claimed to identify a number of faults in Labour groups, among them "conduct falling below the highest standards expected", "factional and dysfunctional Labour groups", "long-standing majoritarianism providing the basis for complacency" and "a failure to provide leadership of the necessary modernisation of local government". There was no reference to the fact that the selection of Labour councillors and the policies followed by Labour councils have been controlled by Millbank for some time. Instead, Millbank's argument went like this: some Labour councillors are (or may be) corrupt; we in New Labour are against corruption; therefore any Labour councillors proved to be corrupt must be Old Labour and against our "modernising agenda"; therefore anybody who is against our "modernising agenda" is likely to be corrupt. In Doncaster, the councillors brought in by Millbank supposedly to clear up the mess have themselves been convicted of corrupt practices. During the discussion, Prescott described Doncaster as "a lot of fuss about a few sandwiches", somehow ignoring the fact that councillors had been convicted of criminal offences. Christine and I voted against the paper.

We next came to a seemingly innocuous paper headed "Making the NEC Work Better", which was introduced by Maggie Jones (trade union representative from UNISON, who had been elected Vice-Chair of the Party in October 1999 and became Chair of the Party in October 2000). Although one of the paper's recommendations was that papers should be sent out in advance, this one was laid around at the meeting itself. Quickly skimming it, I realised that this paper was far from innocuous. "The conduct of NEC meetings is the issue which continues to attract the most concern," the paper claimed. "There is a tendency for the NEC to conduct long debates on some items which then squeezes the time available for other, equally important, issues. This in turn raises the issue of how do individual NEC members measure their contribution to the NEC and how does the NEC as a whole value them." This was all code for an assertion that the Grassroots Alliance was hijacking the agenda of the NEC, and engaging the majority in pointless long debates. That felt rather ironic given the repeated practice of the NEC of moving to next business whenever we put motions. Jones recommended that "the debate following the contribution by the Leader of the Labour Party should be restricted to the key issues facing the government and the Party" and "there should not be a presumption on speaking rights on every issue". She finished with a lecture: "Ultimately, individual NEC members should measure their success by what contribution they have made to helping the Party achieve its objective."

Having failed to prevent the Grassroots Alliance being elected to the NEC, they were now trying to prevent us speaking at it. When Maggie Jones complained about "people who come here and don't do a good deal else", I presume she was referring to us. As we were just about the only people there not in paid full-time labour movement or political jobs, this was a bit rich. The Chair proposed to agree the report without any debate. I said that I wanted to speak against the report and was backed up by Diana Holland. The Chair quickly said that the report should be noted (not agreed) and brought back to the next meeting.

Finally, we came to the item on the London mayor. At this point, yet another report was laid round, and once again there was no time to study it. Among other things, it declared that the ballot papers for selection of the Labour candidate would go out on 26 January and the ballot would close on 16 February 2000. Christine asked why the timetable had slipped, but received no answer. Introducing the report, McDonagh said that they would prefer that trade unions balloted their members, but there was no requirement to do so. The paper stated that eligible trade unions were those "affiliated to the London Labour Party as of 31st December 1998", eligible Party members were those who were paid up on or before 24 September 1999, and eligible MPs, MEPs and GLA candidates were those who were endorsed on or before 24 September 1999.

There were substantial implications for the outcome of the selection in all of these details. It was common knowledge that, even with the device of an electoral college, the selection was on a knife edge and every vote mattered. Following the 12 October NEC meeting at which the selection procedure was agreed, the London Labour Party had calculated which trade unions were affiliated "as of 31st December 1998". Four trade unions – London

Regional MSF, London RMT, ASLEF, and the National League for the Blind and Disabled – had traditionally paid their subscriptions to the London Labour Party later than others, but these subscriptions had always been accepted and the unions had always been entitled to participate in the business of the London Party (such as sending delegates to London Conferences). For the year ending 31 December 1998, London Region MSF had sent a cheque in July 1999 – late, but before the electoral college had been decided. The London Labour Party had acknowledged receipt and had indeed cashed the cheque. The other three had either paid later than July, or were still in arrears. Nobody thought much about it until the London Labour Party came to calculate the eligible trade unions for the purposes of the mayoral selection. It so happened that the four trade unions that paid late were all expected to back Livingstone. The contest was looking extremely close, and every vote would matter. Had it been the AEEU that sent in a late payment, Party officials would, I think, have been extremely unlikely to exclude them from any ballots. Both Mark and I challenged McDonagh's recommendation that the London Region MSF should be excluded and pointed out that the cheque sent in July 1999 had been cashed and not refunded to the union. It seemed a bit much to take the money and then deny them their basic rights. Margaret Wall, the MSF representative on the NEC, said not a word.

Six members of London Region MSF, including Jim Mortimer, former General Secretary of the Labour Party, later challenged this decision and took the Labour Party to court. They were subjected to serious pressure from the national executive of the MSF, which tried to prevent them taking the case. Three of them were suspended from holding office in the union. It was claimed against them that they put union funds at risk – although they funded the court case themselves. Roger Lyons, General Secretary of MSF, provided a witness statement for the Labour Party to use in court, to the effect that these individuals had no right to bring this case. New officers of London Region MSF, who had nothing to do with the court case, were subsequently also suspended from office. At the time of writing, three members of London Region

MSF (two of whom were among the claimants in the court case, and one who was not) remain suspended but have yet to face disciplinary proceedings. One of them, Sue Michie, was voted by MSF members onto their national executive *after* she had been suspended from holding office and therefore in protest at the suspension, but the MSF national executive has refused to allow her to attend meetings.

We did achieve one success at the NEC. To participate in the "payroll" section, GLA candidates had to have been endorsed by 24 September 1999. The fourteen constituency candidates had been endorsed by the NEC on 21 September 1999 and were therefore eligible. The eleven top-up candidates, however, were due to be endorsed at this very meeting. I pointed this out, and obtained McDonagh's agreement that the top-up candidates could not participate in the payroll section. The eleven top-up candidates were headed by Trevor Phillips, running as Dobson's deputy, and were New Labourites through and through. So I felt that for once I had been able to achieve something practical – reducing some of Dobson's built-in advantage. Hidden away in the paper was a requirement that the votes of the "payroll" section be recorded; it was assumed this would deter any MP or MEP who might be tempted to vote for Livingstone in a secret ballot.

Both Helen Jackson and Mary Turner raised the question of access to membership lists. Dobson's mailings to London Labour Party members had received considerable press attention by that time, and people were asking where he had obtained the lists from. His explanations kept shifting. At first he said that he was given lists of local Party members by London MPs who were supporting his campaign. This explanation was blown out of the water when members of Islington North, Hackney North and Stoke Newington, Brent East and Hampstead and Highgate con-stituency parties received mailings. Jeremy Corbyn and Diane Abbott were unlikely to have given Dobson lists of their constitu-ency members, and Ken Livingstone and Glenda Jackson had certainly not done so. Dobson then said that he had had lists from one or more of the London Labour MEPs.

McDonagh looked the NEC straight in the eye and said:

"Millbank and the GLLP gave no data about members at all." She denied that Party members were unhappy about receiving mailings and said that Millbank had received complaints not about mailings but about an advert by "a certain candidate" (Millbank-speak for Livingstone). In my report on the NEC for *Tribune*, I described what she said as a "categorical assurance" that neither Millbank nor the London Labour Party had passed on membership lists to the Dobson campaign. McDonagh never took issue with my description of her remarks.

On 13 December 1999, *Panorama* broadcast an investigation into the London mayoral selection, and the truth behind the membership lists was revealed. Dobson was interviewed, claiming that he had "access to a number of lists, at least one full one". He said that he had never inquired who had provided any of the lists. *Panorama* uncovered a report from a Party member who had been telephone-canvassed by the Dobson campaign. When the member asked where the campaign had got the phone number from, the canvasser named Richard Balfe and another MEP. *Panorama* said that the second MEP was Claude Moraes. Both Balfe and Moraes are London MEPs.

It was said that the requests for membership lists had come to Millbank on the two MEPs' behalf early in October 1999. One wonders why these two MEPs had been so keen to acquire membership lists of the London Labour Party at that particular time. *Panorama* reported that Moraes's assistant, Linda Smith, had asked Millbank for the list after Dobson had declared his candidacy. Linda Smith is a New Labour councillor in Hackney and was on secondment from her paid job with Moraes to work for the Dobson campaign. *Panorama* went on to say that Linda Smith had been told by Millbank that the list would take some time to produce. According to *Panorama*, the General Secretary, Margaret McDonagh, was then contacted and asked if she could help. The request was then prioritised. The list was put onto disk and the disks were sent to Linda Smith at Claude Moraes's office. Smith took them straight to Dobson headquarters, not even bothering to keep a copy for Moraes. The list was never seen by Moraes and never used in his work as an MEP. Richard Balfe, the first MEP

named by *Panorama*, was said to have asked Millbank for a print-
out of the London membership list himself, again in early
October 1999 and after Dobson had declared. His request had
been processed by Jackie Stacey, the Head of Operations, who
reports to the General Secretary. Balfe's involvement showed a
particular irony, and a thick skin. In November 1999, he had
written to *Tribune* saying that one of the reasons he supported
Dobson was because he had received a mailing from Dobson and
not from the other candidates.

Panorama had written to McDonagh setting out the sequence of
events. The reporter read out her response. She claimed that the
MEPs were entitled to the membership list. It was their constitutional and automatic right. She also denied that she had received
any phone call requesting that the production of the list be
expedited, but said that there was a phone call to Jackie Stacey.
On 29 December 1999, Jackson and Livingstone submitted a
dossier of complaints to the scrutineer, Unity Security Ballots (see
Appendix 3). Neither USB nor the Labour Party ever investigated
the complaints.

Away from the London contest, skirmishes with Millbank continued on other issues. I had attended the Organisation Sub-
committee to speak to the rule changes that I had proposed at
the July NEC – the "Sawyer" and "Cashman" amendments and the
establishment of fixed dates for the NEC ballot (see Chapter 6). I
was aware that I was just going through the motions, but if I did
not attend, I would have been accused of not being serious about
the amendments. The Organisation Sub-committee listened to
me with a mixture of amusement and contempt. Anne Picking
accused me of being motivated against "two particular members
of the NEC". I replied that both Cashman's and Sawyer's present
positions on the NEC were in my opinion unjustifiable – but that
in any case my amendments would not apply to them, as they
were not intended to have retrospective effect. The proposals
were defeated unanimously – since I was not entitled to a vote
and the one supporter of the Grassroots Alliance who sat on the
Organisation Sub-committee, Dennis Skinner, was ill and could
not attend.

The Times picked up the story about the "Making the NEC Work Better" document, which it ran as "Labour's NEC to silence Left troublemakers". It described the proposals as being designed to ensure that left-wingers would be "seen but not heard". Blair, *The Times* reported, regarded his attendance at the NEC as "an ordeal" and it was said that we "harangued" him. For the record, the Prime Minister was required to listen to our questions for a grand total of about five minutes once every two months. *The Times* named Maggie Jones as the author of the paper – a passing reference she later described as "a personal attack".

The National Policy Forum met for a weekend at Eastbourne. No decisions were to be made or votes taken; it was all sitting in workshops and discussing the policy documents. At a dinner on the Saturday evening, Tony Robinson was the after-dinner comic turn. Robinson is a fully paid-up Blairite and, with Michael Cashman, had been involved in a Blairite take-over of the Equity national executive. By now, the rumours were stronger than ever that Robinson would be Millbank's celebrity candidate for the NEC in 2000 – and the frequency of his appearances at Party events tended to confirm these rumours. In Eastbourne, Robinson treated the National Policy Forum delegates to a number of jokes including some at the expense of Christine and myself – along the lines of how "far left" we were. I was happy to laugh, but Christine understandably saw the whole thing as shameless electioneering for the NEC and refused to join in. As usual, the Grassroots Alliance sat together at the dinner, partly to huddle together for warmth, partly because most delegates were scared to be seen talking to us. Prescott made a tour of the tables, but as he headed towards ours, he clocked who was sitting there and changed direction fast.

8

The London Stitch-up

For a variety of reasons, I decided over Christmas 1999 that I would not stand again for the National Executive Committee. I was finding it increasingly difficult to give the NEC – and with it the job of providing one of the public faces of the Labour left – the attention it deserved. For eight years I had been a Labour councillor. Immediately after that, I had thrown myself into the NEC election campaign and was now in the middle of my second year as an NEC member. Throughout all this time, I also had to work at my full-time jobs, at first as a solicitor and then as a barrister. I was very weary of juggling what felt like two full-time jobs.

I also could not face the thought of being on the NEC during the general election campaign. I realised I could no longer honestly and publicly describe myself as a supporter of this government. Taken as a whole, its record on asylum, civil liberties, privatisation, cuts in welfare provision, its attacks on the poor, its subservience to big business, and its willingness to bomb people in other countries had made that impossible. As it happens, because I live in the Hackney North constituency, I will be voting Labour in the next general election because I strongly support the work of my local left-wing Labour MP, Diane Abbott. But I will certainly not be voting for Tony Blair and if I lived in a constituency in which the Labour candidate was a Blairite, I could not advocate a vote for the Party in which I have spent my entire adult life. In those circumstances, how could I put myself forward to Party members as a candidate for the NEC? Events since that Christmas have only confirmed the decision I took then.

On 13 January 2000, the London Region MSF case came to court. The London Region MSF officers had a simple argument based on contract: there was custom and practice that they paid their subscriptions to the London Labour Party late and they had never been prohibited from participating in the activity of the London Party in the past; in cashing the cheque for affiliation fees in August 1999 the London Labour Party had waived the failure to pay during 1998 and therefore accepted their affiliation for that year. The Labour Party argued that payment was required by 31 December 1998. The judge took the view, as judges usually do, that by and large the Party had the right to regulate its own affairs and could interpret its own rules in this way if it saw fit. (Later that year, at Conference in October, the Party agreed a rule change requiring trade unions to pay their affiliations during the year for which they are affiliated and not later; the need for this change in wording rather confirmed that the rule had not been as clear-cut as Millbank had previously claimed.) So London Region MSF – and the other three unions – could not participate in the mayoral ballot. Had they been able to do so, Livingstone might have won.

The NEC met on 25 January. The papers sent out in advance included an update from Maggie Jones on "Making the NEC Work Better". Millbank had backed down. Restrictions on what we could ask the Prime Minister had been dropped, as were the comments about there being no presumption of speaking rights and about how the "success" of an NEC member should be measured. There remained some gentle hints that restrictions might be implemented in the future: "A recognition of the authority of the Chair to guide the NEC through the agenda may mean, at times, moving the debate on before everyone has been called to speak. If this works effectively there is no need to have the more rigid solution of timed agendas." Yet again, on the morning of the NEC, extracts from the paper had appeared in the press.

Vernon Hince opened the meeting by telling us that we should be "more loyal, not less" and complaining that the NEC agenda had been printed in several national newspapers. Blair delivered his usual homilies. Complaints about the media ("there's been a concerted press onslaught against the government"), attacks on the Tories ("their answer is private health") and grumblings about Party members ("We are in for a period of the press trying to bring us down. I'm amazed that Labour Party members don't know that. We must use the next period for campaigning messages."). I asked him to reconsider the proposed 1p tax cut and use the revenue instead to increase health spending – and congratulated him on his welcome pledge, on *Breakfast with Frost*, to increase health spending to the European average. He replied that he "felt nervous" being congratulated by me, that health spending would increase but the NHS needed to be "reformed" at the same time. He clearly preferred Margaret Wall's question. Noting how "pleased" she was that "you reminded us of the Tories' position on private health", she asked, "How can we get the campaigning message out? How can we do that work?"

I also asked Blair to drop the Mode of Trial Bill (restricting the right to trial by jury) which had just been defeated in the Lords. He said that the Bill would release £100 million for "front-line policing" and was "a law and order issue". Christine asked about the "modernising local government" proposals which had been rejected in a unanimous vote by Camden Labour councillors. Blair said that he wouldn't answer the question, suspecting that there was "a trick in it" that he could not see. Hilary Armstrong took up the cudgels, saying that "modernising local government" – local councils conducting business through small cabinets meeting in secret – was a more flexible system than the present system and that the present system was brought in "before you or I, Christine, or many men had the vote. Local government then was for the landed gentry. Our system is clear accountability and transparency."

Dennis Skinner, back to the NEC after illness, referred laconically to "a problem with the London mayor". He put the case for increasing the minimum wage and spending more on the NHS, to show clear dividing lines between Labour and the Tories. He was backed up by Mary Turner of the GMB, who urged the government to "give a little to those at the bottom". In response,

Blair compared New Labour's position with that of the Tories in 1982. Skinner interrupted that in 1983, Thatcher had the Falklands. Blair joked, "Well, we don't need to do that yet." He ended up with the usual whinge. "There are so-called Labour supporters saying, what's the government ever done for us? But we must never forget what will happen if the Tories get in. Look at the 1970s. The Labour government fell out with itself and we ended up with a right-wing Tory government. The Tories are now more right-wing than ever, even than they were under Thatcher. There are no constraints on their right wing. There is no restraining influence. If people are critical, they should look at what we've done. What the press believe is that they have only three or four months to get the Tories off the ground. The editors are very frustrated with the Tories. They are not used to Labour governing competently or to the Tories falling apart. Tories in opposition are used to attacking the government and waiting for the government to fall into their lap. As Dennis Skinner said, we must keep the dividing lines in mind. That must be understood by the entirety of the Labour Party. If that's not in place within the Labour Party, we will never get the public to understand."

Blair then left and we came to McDonagh's report. The NEC ballot this year was to take place between 26 April and 17 May – even earlier than the previous year and timed to coincide with local elections in England. There was to be a grand centenary celebration, televised by Sky, and a centenary dinner, and selected long-serving members would be invited to Number Ten. I asked McDonagh about the revelations on the *Panorama* programme, including the report that the request for the London members' list was activated after a phone call made either to her or to the Head of Operations, Jackie Stacey. I also asked whether Blair's meetings, dedicated to promoting Dobson and savaging Livingstone, would be included in Dobson's election expenses. Helen Jackson said that everybody believed that the result would be close, and would leave virtually half the London Labour Party feeling bruised and hurt. What plans did McDonagh have to pull the London Labour Party together in order to win the mayoral election in May? Jeuda complained that the NEC elections were too early, leaving candidates with little time to campaign. Vernon Hince responded that we were all responsible for NEC decisions and so Diana should not complain about dates.

Eventually, McDonagh offered a reply to my question. "Neither I nor any member of staff would directly or indirectly knowingly give lists to one candidate's campaign. I wouldn't tell you one thing and do another. People in the organisation have rights of access to the list. I don't have the right not to give those people lists. I feel very frustrated that someone who has the right to the list should have to ring up and ask for it. In the next few weeks, they will be able to do it by computer. If Claude Moraes had rung up and asked for the list, I would have made sure he got it. He didn't. But I would have given it to him. The only information is based on the press. I didn't watch *Panorama*." She added: "It's right that this caused a lot of upset in the membership. That needs to be addressed through the discussion on 'The 21st Century Party'. It's in some people's political interest to ensure belief in a conspiracy." As far as Blair's meetings were concerned, she said, these were part of a programme of meetings all over the country; just a minority of questions were about the London mayor, and therefore they could not be charged to Dobson's campaign. The next day's *Independent* would contain the following account of McDonagh's reply: "McDonagh conceded that members were upset and said that the leadership was right to listen to them . . . said that she was happy to have a debate about future elections and raised the prospect of new rules being included in plans to modernise Labour's internal structures." It appears that, some time after the NEC meeting had finished, somebody in Millbank decided that this was the message they wanted spun to the press, an ambiguous message of conciliation, quite different from McDonagh's actual words, which were far from conciliatory.

Later in the meeting, the paper on the dates for the NEC election was put by the Chair to the NEC "for information". Diana Jeuda, who had left the meeting for a while after her criticism of the dates and had now returned, abandoned her protest, saying that she now accepted the paper. There was a brief discussion, led by Ian McCartney, on the strategy for the general election, which most people expected would be held in 2001. Most of the discussion concerned how to motivate Party activists, and it ended up as a skirmish over "The 21st Century Party" document. Derek Hodgson said, "We've lost foot soldiers. We have to address traditional voters. The jury's out on some political issues." Jeremy Beecham warned on pensions: "the politics of the 75p increase are difficult and will be played against us". Others defended the "21st Century Party" process. Jeuda said that the process involved activists and that activists were "tired". McDonagh laid down the New Labour law: "It's not the case that there's a difference between the core vote and the new 1997 voters. There was a swing to us because we were New Labour. The reason we did poorly was in areas where we were delivering Old Labour policies." Ian McCartney defended "The 21st Century Party": "it's about empowering activists", "about rebuilding and modernising the [trade union] link". He then went on to complain: "it's not surprising there is cynicism if you go around attacking the government. If you attack the leadership, you shouldn't complain. We have to go around clearing up the lies, innuendoes, mistruths." So the groundwork for any scapegoating that might need to be done after the next general election was being laid early.

Finally, we came to the "Making the NEC Work Better" document. Maggie Jones complained that she had not envisaged that it would be so controversial. She admitted that she had received a number of written and verbal submissions on her document, but gave no details. To the best of my knowledge, the only written comments she had were from Mark and from me, both opposing the document. In Millbank's usual defensive way, the discussion (on what was now a fairly innocuous paper) turned into a series of attacks on the Grassroots Alliance, in particular our reports of NEC meetings in *Tribune*, in *Labour Left Briefing* and in our bulletins. Jeremy Beecham said that members of the NEC felt inhibited from asking questions when they knew that those questions would be published. Clive Soley asked, "What sort of NEC is this? . . . Are we elected representatives to answer questions and report back?" It wasn't clear what else he thought we were or should be.

I defended the Grassroots Alliance's right to publish accounts of the meetings: we were elected on an unequivocal commitment to report back and that's what we would do. The NEC was not a cabinet or consultative forum; it was the governing body of a major national political party, and its members had to be accountable to those who elected them. At least we were open and honest about publishing these accounts, whereas I frequently read reports in the newspapers on my way to the NEC of laid-round papers that I had not even seen. Simon Murphy (newly elected Leader of the European Parliamentary Labour Party, replacing Alan Donnelly, who had resigned as an MEP at the end of 1999) said that if I had made those comments on Walsall Council, the leader would have "had my guts for garters". Jones said that she objected to the Party membership reading accounts of its own NEC in *Tribune* or the *Independent*. It was not clear whether she thought any of our deliberations should be published anywhere.

The ballot for Labour candidate for London mayor closed on 16 February and Ken Livingstone gave a party. Officially Livingstone and his supporters were up-beat, but Livingstone was saying privately that he had been told that he had lost by 3 per cent. On 20 February, the world learned that Livingstone had indeed lost by 3 per cent. It was uncanny how accurate the leaks turned out to be. I went out that lunchtime, arriving home to find a message from Vernon Hince on my answerphone informing me that Dobson had won. My phone rang all afternoon. Party members were fuming. Dobson had won because the AEEU and the CWS, who between them commanded 8 per cent of the electoral college, cast their votes for him without balloting their own members. In addition, Pauline Green, who was no longer a London MEP (and had moved to Manchester), had a vote in the payroll section worth 0.4 per cent of the total – and had voted for Dobson. On the final figures (after distribution of Glenda Jackson's 4 per cent of the vote), Party members had voted 59.9 per cent for Livingstone and 40.1 per cent for Dobson. Trade unions had voted 72 per cent for Livingstone and 26.9 per cent for Dobson. The politicians section divided 86.5 per cent for Dobson and 13.5 per cent for Livingstone. Had the four excluded trade unions been allowed to participate (and had they all voted for Livingstone), Livingstone would have won. It wasn't just Livingstone who had been robbed; it was every Labour Party and trade union member in London.

Time and time again that afternoon Party members, by no means all left-wingers, told me that Livingstone should stand as an independent and that they would support him. It takes a lot for Party members to come to that view. The general convention in the Party is that after a selection contest, whoever has won, a line is drawn and everybody campaigns together for the successful candidate. But this was different. Livingstone was the clear winner in the two democratic sections of the electoral college. The result was nothing but a fix. I told Channel 4 News that Party members were "fuming". The reporter described this comment as "the furthest" that any Party member would go in public.

For two weeks, Livingstone played a wait-and-see game. Dobson was looking weaker and weaker. He urged Livingstone on *Question Time* to "make my day" but couldn't quite summon up the conviction of Clint Eastwood. Millbank's control-freakery backfired again when they tried to organise parliamentary researchers and other Blairites to attend *Question Time* in order to jeer at Livingstone; the email divulging this plan was leaked to the press. Labour Party meetings and trade union branches all over London passed motions calling on Dobson to stand down, and to acknowledge Livingstone as the winner and the Party's official candidate. Five days after *Question Time*, on 6 March, Livingstone declared his independent candidacy. Somewhat bizarrely, he had called a meeting that evening for Labour Party members to discuss what he should do. But when he announced his candidacy, the meeting was cancelled.

Livingstone's announcement forced a crisis for many London Labour Party members, and for the left of the Party in general. Formally, supporting any candidate standing against an official Labour Party candidate is grounds for expulsion from the Party. Livingstone was dissuading Party members from working for him too publicly, arguing that people should remain in the Party to campaign for his return. Millbank told the press that disciplinary action would not be taken against Party members who supported Livingstone – but as with so much of Millbank's spin, Party members could not be sure if this was true. Nonetheless, many took the risk of publicly supporting Livingstone. In the end, the only disciplinary proceedings were against Livingstone himself. It had dawned on Millbank that it was unwise to inflame Labour Party members any further.

Some Party members (including my partner, an active member for twenty years) left the Party and publicly supported both Livingstone and the London Socialist Alliance, which was standing candidates for the Greater London Assembly. Some worked quietly for Livingstone and/or the London Socialist Alliance. Public figures on the left of the Party stayed quiet, and let Livingstone get on with the show. Whilst the question of whether to support Livingstone openly was a complicated one, and divided the left, there was a near-unanimous refusal amongst Party members of all shades to work for Dobson. It was probably the most solid "strike" by Labour's foot soldiers ever seen.

The NEC met on 28 March. We were on the eve of the first democratic election for London government for nineteen years. The Party was running for mayor a candidate with negligible popular support. The likely winner, streets ahead in the polls, was a dissident left-wing independent. These were extraordinary circumstances, by any measure, but for most people at the New Labour NEC, it was business as usual. Gordon Brown turned up to tell us about the budget. "The Labour Party is making economic efficiency a platform for social justice"; the government "aspired" to full employment, and intended to "tackle" child and pensioner poverty. In light of that year's 75p per week increase in pensions, the intention sounded hollow. Brown argued that "if we simply raised pensions in line with earnings, we could not have put money into pensioner poverty". Blair backed him up: "the tactics of our opponents is to make people cynical, so that they say that all politicians are all smoke and mirrors." Then Blair returned to his favourite culprits: "the media will always prefer a Tory government to a Labour government".

I asked Brown (to whom questions were supposed to be

directed) why the minimum wage had not been increased by more than 10p, so that employers would pay for lifting people out of poverty. Ignoring the direction of the Chair, I also asked Blair if he would support Dobson doing "the honourable thing" and standing down. I warned that the Party faced a rout at the ballot box and that it was not too late to intervene. Other members of the NEC were also critical, though in more circumspect terms. Jeuda said, "People are frightened by the suggestion that benefits might be taken away from them." Mike Griffiths said, "Some industrial problems are made in Britain rather than globally. Manufacturing can do no more than wait for the inevitable turn. We hope for change." This was code for saying that interest rates should be lowered. Mary Turner talked about the fear of privatisation of residential homes, and, in relation to the selling off of state assets, complained, "when you sell off the family jewels you have no control". She said that any moves to sell off council housing would be a big issue in the general and local elections: "it's not true that private is best". Dennis Skinner hoped that privatisation of air traffic control would be shelved.

Simon Murphy claimed that people were oversimplifying the situation in the car industry, which was the result of a catastrophic failure by BMW management (and therefore nothing to do with the government). Jeremy Beecham complained about the government's proposals to channel money directly to schools and other designated services, rather than allowing local government to allocate the money. He had been quoted four days earlier in the *Independent* warning Blunkett of "stormy water" ahead if school funding powers were removed from councils. He even handed round photocopies of the *Independent* story, insisting with a self-deprecating smile that he had "never imagined" that his quote would be so prominent.

Blair replied that the car industry was "a potentially serious situation". The government had "an active strategy" and was working "to limit the damage". But he ruled out intervention on lower interest rates – "intervening artificially to bring the pound down will create more problems". He told me that the minimum wage had been increased (a nonresponse to my question) and that on "London": "The honourable thing would have been to abide by the electoral result." He repeated the untruth that the selection ballot had used the same electoral college that elected him and Prescott. As for pensioners, they would "want more, but it's hard to say that we haven't done anything". He ignored the specific questions on privatisation of residential homes, council housing, and air traffic control and returned to the Tories: "the Tory strategy is to disillusion people – so that they say that they are all the same and so they put back the Tories". It seemed a bit rich to blame the Tories for stoking cynicism about politics when the Labour Party had just been through a selection process in which the candidate for whom the clear majority voted was not declared the winner.

Brown listed the government's achievements: an increase in child benefit, "lifting pensioners out of poverty", reducing the base rate of tax by 1p. He rejected the philosophy of intervention: "We are undergoing a period of restructuring. There's been a long-term neglect of investment. We provide the opportunities to stay in industry or the skills to move. We cannot return to boom and bust. If we lowered the currency, we would return to boom and bust. Hundreds of thousands of jobs would go if we dipped into a real recession." He then launched into some statistics from Peter Kilfoyle's Liverpool constituency – how many families had received increases in child benefit and so forth. This sounded more like a soundbite for a question raised in Parliament than a response to the criticisms actually raised at the NEC – and indeed it had been used in Parliament in response to Kilfoyle's resignation speech the previous day in which he had accused the government of not delivering for his constituents. Brown concluded with the ritual injunction: "our duty is to get the message out".

The Chair thanked him, observing, "our founders would be ecstatic if they knew what was said this morning". A vision of Keir Hardie celebrating a less than one per cent increase in the basic state pension in the midst of an economic boom sprang to mind. Hince went on to echo Blair and Brown: "our opponents are not the Tories but the media".

The main item of NEC business was a presentation on the ongoing London election campaign by Jim Fitzpatrick (MP for Newham and Chair of the London Labour Party) and David Evans (Assistant General Secretary of the Party). These two were being set up to take the flak for Labour's inevitably disastrous result. They told us that the campaign would be "tough and difficult" but that "the electorate is sophisticated enough to reward political loyalty and punish political cowardice". Their game plan was to promote "Frank, the man". Although Dobson enjoyed a high degree of public recognition, he was not yet widely understood "as a person . . . so we're getting very personal".

Christine said that we were fighting with not one, but two hands tied behind our back. She warned that the section on the London underground in the election manifesto "could lose you the election". Dianne Hayter interrupted her to say, "We, Christine, we, not you." Christine replied that she was talking about the government's policy and of course she would be delivering leaflets for Dobson – which she later did. I had no intention of delivering leaflets for Dobson and would have had said so if asked (although I admit I was not going to volunteer the information).

The spectacle of grown women and men trying to convince themselves that Livingstone was beatable was tragicomic. Beecham opined that Frank Dobson's main strength was "working with people", unlike Ken Livingstone. Clive Soley said, "The feeling on the door is difficult, but not as much as some think . . . there's a problem with voting for Livingstone and people know that's true. He was not prepared to stand on the Labour Party manifesto – not just the tube but unwilling to commit himself to the manifesto. He didn't declare that he had a company worth £220,000. That was all about his willingness to run as an independent. He has the tactics and strategy of the GLC days rather than anything else. He had the same problem as the miners did – the cause was right but the tactics disastrous." Solely concluded, "There was a problem with the selection process. That problem was Ken Livingstone and his personal ambition." Prescott said that Dobson should be praised for carrying out the Party's public–private partnership policy on the tube. Ian McCartney said that Dobson, unlike Livingstone, was "fighting for Londoners not for himself". Fitzpatrick said that one of Dobson's strengths was that he was "more friendly to business" and had endorsement from business. But Fitzpatrick admitted, "It's a hard task because of the media view of the campaign." David Evans joined in the carping: "There's a political decision from the media not to carry Labour Party analysis and rebuttal. We have to be very agile in a hostile media environment." He was particularly pleased that the Police Federation had endorsed Dobson and, glancing at Christine and me, said that the Party intended to expose "our opponent" (Livingstone) but that he couldn't say any more about that at the moment.

There was a much shorter discussion on the local elections in the rest of Britain, in which, once again, everyone except Millbank was blamed for the stuttering campaign. "Where people vote for Liberals," McDonagh explained, "they are voting against Labour, and that's where they have crap Labour councils."

I proposed a motion (seconded by Mark and Christine) that in future electoral colleges, trade unions could only participate if they balloted their members, and urging a reconsideration of the weighted votes given to elected representatives. The Millbank staffers went into a tizzy. On the one hand, the last thing they wanted to do was to concede any democratic clout to the base of the trade union movement; trade union leaders remain far easier to manipulate than trade union members who (in London, at least) have a nasty habit of voting for left-wing candidates. On the other hand, it had finally dawned on them that the handling of the London selection had discredited the Labour Party and alienated both members and voters; they were anxious to be seen to do something. They asked me if the motion could be referred to the 21st Century Party consultation. Mindful of what had happened to every other motion referred to a consultation process or sub-committee or review, I refused. If Millbank was prepared to concede on trade union ballots, they would do so whether or not our motion went to the 21st Century Party consultation.

When I spoke to the motion, I finally got the chance to point out that the electoral college used in Wales and London was not the same as the one that elected Blair and Prescott; it was something to have got that off my chest, after listening to the Prime Minister, among other Party leaders, spout disinformation on this question for months. The fact that the weighted votes cast by elected representatives had overturned the clear majority opinion in the other two sections had discredited the whole process. I said that after this experience Party members desperately needed a message of reassurance now. Christine and Mark backed me up. Anne Picking said she was very angry: what right had we got to tell the trade unions what to do? We were "malicious". Hodgson said this was a waste of time and demanded we go straight to the vote. McCartney said that we were "engaging in tactics for and against candidates". Prescott at least acknowledged the problem: "ordinary Labour Party members think they have been done over by Millbank. We all know some things happen." But he also said that if this resolution were passed, it would be interpreted as "damaging the Party". Cashman remarked that at best the motion was "naïve", at worst it was "mischievous and would undermine the Labour candidate". I repeated that Party members needed reassurance now. The motion was defeated by twenty-two votes to three.

General chaos then ensued. Both Ian McCartney and Diana Jeuda were saying that the motion should now be referred to the 21st Century Party consultation. Vernon Hince ruled that the motion had been defeated and so it could not be referred anywhere. Hodgson asked McDonagh if the scope of the 21st Century Party consultation could be broadened and she said yes, it could. Thus the motion was (sort of) referred to the 21st Century Party consultation, even though it had been rejected by the NEC.

As everyone except the Labour NEC majority had predicted, the London election was a disaster for Labour. Livingstone swept home. Across the city, there was hardly a window poster to be seen in support of Dobson. Most London MPs avoided being seen with him. Even Blair got edgy about campaigning for him. And the chosen campaign themes only further alienated Party members. Dobson described himself as the "pro-police, pro-business" candidate, endorsed New Labour's attacks on beggars and asylum seekers; he hit rock bottom when he tried to link Livingstone with what he called the "thuggery" of the May Day "riot" by anti-capitalist protesters in London. Labour voters stayed at home or voted for alternatives. Turnout was only 34 per cent, for one of the most publicised and controversial elections in British history. Disenchantment showed itself in the huge vote for Livingstone and the increased votes for the smaller parties: the Greens, the British National Party (frighteningly), the Christian People's Alliance, and the various left alternatives (London Socialist Alliance, Campaign Against Tube Privatisation, Peter Tatchell).

Personally, I took great pleasure in voting for Livingstone and for the London Socialist Alliance. But I was left more unhappy than ever with the dilemmas I had been wrestling with over Christmas, and that had led me to stand down from the NEC.

9

Millbank Unrepentant

Three days before the London and local elections, I was one of the speakers at Burnley Trades Council's year 2000 May Day march and rally. It was an honour to be invited – especially because I had links with the town, unknown to the trades council. My mother had grown up in Burnley and as a child I had regularly visited my grandmother there. The other speakers were the local MP, Peter Pike; Gordon Prentice, the MP for the neighbouring constituency of Pendle; and Bruce Kent, the well-known campaigner and spokesperson for CND. The attendance was modest but enthusiastic – and uniformly hostile to New Labour. There were cheers for the Chair, a veteran local trade unionist, when he denounced the government for wanting to create an economy "where half the population are selling insurance to or cutting the hair of the other half", and again when he announced that the anti-capitalist protesters in London had closed off Parliament Square (these were cheers from a very traditional labour movement audience). Both MPs took great pains to persuade the crowd that they should get out and vote Labour that week – persuasion that would not normally have been necessary in Burnley, a heartland Labour area. Gordon Prentice delivered one of the sharpest critiques of the government I've heard – and finished by reasserting that the real "big ideas" for our time were progressive taxation and the redistribution of wealth. When he declared that he would not vote for privatisation of air traffic control, he was warmly applauded.

After spending the day with activists in Burnley, listening to their discontent, and their reports of the election campaign, I was not surprised when, a few days later, in Burnley as in other working-class constituencies, Labour support dipped to its lowest level in living memory. Everywhere, voter turnout was down. Millbank had calculated that the loss of 200 council seats was inevitable, but wanted to restrict the numbers of lost seats to between 200 and 400. Anything over 400 losses would be seen as an indication of Tory recovery. On the night, Labour lost 566 seats, and lost control of nineteen councils, including Burnley.

During these weeks, the ballot for the six constituency places on the National Executive Committee was also taking place, amid even less public awareness than the previous year. The ballot papers were mailed out inside the Party's official magazine *Inside Labour* – a largely unread corporate-style in-house journal full of puff pieces for cabinet members and exhortations to "campaign". Many copies were undoubtedly deposited in the bin unopened, and with them the NEC ballot papers. On top of that, the Party's membership department (outsourced since January) was in chaos. Membership applications and renewals weren't being processed and membership cards were late in being sent out. Millbank's claim that Party members would be more likely to vote if the ballot was held in the middle of the election campaign – when there are no formal meetings of the Party – proved baseless. The turnout was only 25 per cent – down from 35 per cent two years earlier, the first year of the new system.

In addition Party membership itself was in decline. Precisely by how much it is difficult to say. It is next to impossible to track down realistic figures for Party membership – Millbank keeps this data close to its chest. In any case, the Party's one remaining national-level democratic exercise – the annual NEC ballot – was clearly involving and motivating fewer and fewer people. It must be said that the Grassroots Alliance itself did little to raise the profile of the ballot.

The results of the 2000 NEC ballot were announced at the NEC held on 23 May, the first following the election setbacks. Blair didn't attend this NEC – it was three days after the new Blair baby had been born – so Prescott deputised for him. Prescott was late, so Mowlam deputised for Prescott. A few minutes before the meeting started, McDonagh took Mark outside. He came back looking a little shocked and said to me, "I'm off the NEC." In fact, he had come fifth overall (and top of the Grassroots Alliance slate), but three men had beaten him and the rules require three of the six constituency places to be held by women. Ann Black and Christine Shawcroft (who were sixth and seventh respectively) were elected from the Grassroots Alliance. Ann Black had been an active member of the National Policy Forum from the Grassroots Alliance since 1998. If the National Policy Forum were an honest process, she would have been one of its leading members. She engaged seriously in the process, reporting to Labour Party members, studying the details of the documents and submissions, and proposing thoughtful amendments. However, since her amendments were on subjects that New Labour did not want discussed, such as restoring the link between pensions and earnings, she was demonised by New Labour. She had spent two years battling to defend the Grassroots Alliance's right just to put amendments to the policy documents, and against the constant procedural manoeuvres to stop us playing our part. Ann describes herself as formerly "on the right" of the Labour Party. She voted for Tony Blair when he stood for Leader in 1994 and for the new Clause IV in 1995. But in 1997 she was shocked at the Partnership in Power proposals to restrict Labour Party democracy, joined Labour Reform and, a year later, was in at the beginning of the Grassroots Alliance.

The Millbank slate took the top four positions. Sawyer was re-elected, despite not having said a word at any of the NEC meetings he had attended. Tony Robinson topped the poll – Millbank's celebrity strategy had paid off. The other two elected were Ruth Turner (who had twice appeared on *Question Time*, thanks to lobbying from Millbank), and Shahid Malik (who had made a name for himself within the Party by claiming local links with a record number of safe Labour seats where there happened to be a parliamentary vacancy). There were a number of reasons for the fallback in the Grassroots Alliance share of the vote, but Mark's campaign wasn't helped by Millbank chopping off the second half of his candidate statement from the official election material – apparently because the staff member typing the statement had failed to turn over the piece of paper.

The NEC began with a tribute to Bernie Grant, MP for Tottenham, who had recently died. The minutes of the previous meeting were altered to say that our motion on selection procedures had been referred to the 21st Century Party consultation. In the real world, the motion had been voted down, and everyone present knew that, but the minutes of these meetings represent reality as Millbank would have us believe it to be, not reality itself. Mowlam announced that in the wake of the local election they were looking for "practical suggestions to improve communications". She mentioned only two concrete initiatives: a press release on drugs had been already sent out, and there was a proposal that ministers should be organised to let Millbank know if they were putting out any announcements, so that Millbank could then brief MPs appropriately.

Prescott arrived and the Party's Polling Co-ordinator gave a presentation on the election results. It was an extraordinarily complacent report. The Romsey by-election was regarded as a "success"; here Labour's vote had decreased from 18.6 per cent (1997) to 3.8 per cent. London was presented as a disaster – for Livingstone. The paper said, "Livingstone's mandate comes from 15.3 per cent of the London electorate." There was no reference to the fact that only 4 per cent of the London electorate could bring themselves to vote for Dobson. The low turnout was attributed to "the 'fear' factor, eg the riots". Whether Millbank imagined that, three days after May Day, electors were scared to venture outside for fear of anti-capitalist protesters, I don't know. Bad results in the English local elections were attributed to local factors – a hospital campaign in Wyre Forest, a road traffic scheme in Oxford. Overall, Millbank considered that this was a good result for a mid-term government. When the officer presenting the report casually described the Birmingham result as being "not too bad", there were mutters that Birmingham was "terrible". After all, even the former leader of the council had lost his seat.

Most NEC members seemed unconvinced by the official line of optimism. Many of these people had direct experience of the lack

of motivation and activity among both members and voters, and
they regarded it as a serious problem. Dianne Hayter said that
there was not enough attention being paid to why people were
not voting – though she was careful to insert a caveat to the effect
that this was the view of the socialist societies, whom she represents, and not necessarily her own. Diana Jeuda talked about the
Liberals winning in Whitby, where they had "no history of activity", and said that the presentation we had just listened to had not
jelled with her experience at all: "Pensions was the issue time and
time again. People were saying that the Labour Party is not the
party for us any more. The core voters don't believe us. . . . We
have to realise that the results were a disaster for the Labour Party
and have to realise that the results were a disaster for the Labour Party
and have a bit of humility."

Christine said that in London the negative campaigning had
turned people off. Dobson's leaflets had not gone down well. "It's
a good thing I'm used to being attacked at these meetings," she
added, "because when I was handing out Dobson leaflets in the
local market, people tore them up and threw them back at us."
Helen Jackson MP said that there was a difference between local
and national elections, but that "we got London wrong" and the
London result, including the Greater London Assembly election,
was bad. Jeremy Beecham was seething. He described the election
result as showing a "real cause for concern". "Greg [the Party's
polling expert] talked about activists and I have to say: what
Labour Party activists? There were fewer people than I've experienced in forty years in the Party. The core workers are usually
councillors, who aren't happy. Pensioners weren't happy."

I said that the paper was not an honest analysis, particularly
about the London result. When I mentioned there being no
Dobson posters anywhere, Prescott interrupted and asked why
there wasn't one in my window. I said that I would have been
embarrassed to put up a Dobson poster – I decided not to
volunteer the information that my partner had put up a London
Socialist Alliance poster. I said that we should realise our mistakes
and readmit Livingstone to the Party. Prescott interrupted again
and said, "What about David Owen then?" Mark was muttering in
a loud voice, "What about Shaun Woodward?" – a reference to

the Conservative MP who had joined Labour some months earlier. Sally Powell said that councillors were feeling unloved by government and relations needed to improve; she complained that Blair was not coming to the local government conference. Mark warned that parts of the electorate had broken the habit of voting Labour. The results were not just about not getting the message across.

Clive Soley was one of the few to echo the official complacency. He said that the Party couldn't just focus on the core vote – "we represent the whole of the country". The low morale of activists was partly about pensions, "but restoring the link with earnings would mean that the poorer pensioners are worse off". He said that London "looked like a fix", but he took no responsibility for that state of affairs, although he had played a prominent role in the process. "Livingstone was always going to be an enormous problem . . . the public like independents. On the doorstep, I had no problem with getting people to join the Labour Party, but there was a problem with getting people out to vote."

Dennis Skinner said there were bad results in 1968 and 1977 "but then the Labour government was skint. This time we have a strong economy." He called for a £5 per week increase in pensions in the forthcoming comprehensive public spending review: "We have a £22 billion windfall and we should use it. Then we have a chance of recovery." Skinner's contribution was welcome, and of course his vote made the diminished Grassroots Alliance presence seem more respectable. But this was not the Dennis Skinner of old. He seemed to have convinced himself that Blair was some kind of new-style Harold Wilson, who just needed a steer in the right direction. Mary Turner of the GMB added, "I could not believe that we're known as the Labour government who gave the lowest rise to pensions." Simon Murphy weighed in on the government's behalf. "75p on pensions was presentationally bad. But with the fuel allowance and TV licence it adds up to £5 per week. These are presentational issues." He was backed up by Ian McCartney who, as previously, complained about the Grassroots Alliance on the NEC: "the leadership is ourselves and we're sending out mixed messages".

Prescott talked promisingly about "humility and honesty", but refused to acknowledge any flaws in government policies. He made no reply to the points on pensions. He agreed that Labour councillors had a perception that "Tony doesn't love us" and said that he was going to the local government conference this year. He added that Blair had been due to attend the conference the previous year, but that he – Prescott – had had to go in his place, "because there had just been the 'scars on the back' comment". Turning to me, he said that the Party had fought in London on the Labour manifesto. Livingstone had got in, but not with a mandate to overturn the manifesto. The £22 billion from mobile phone licences had been spent ten times: "reducing the national debt doesn't sound sexy but it frees up £4 billion to spend".

This discussion of the May election results was the most robust performance by the NEC I witnessed. For once, people were speaking up for those they were elected to represent, giving voice to what was being said at the base of the Labour Party. But I also felt deeply frustrated by the whole scene – because I knew, now, that so little would come of it, and that Millbank's dogmatic insistence that the results had not been a disaster for the Labour Party would prevail.

In an intriguing little spat, Simon Murphy, when speaking to the European Parliamentary Labour Party report, commented on the Rover crisis and the failure of the BMW management to consult the Longbridge workforce. "The German workers could have told the British workers, but they didn't . . ." People were somewhat aghast at this attempt to let the management off the hook and there were cries of "That's outrageous" from all around the table. The Tottenham by-election was looming. Both Mark and Dianne Hayter complained that selecting David Lammy as Labour's candidate, when he had been elected to the Greater London Assembly less than three weeks earlier and was now abandoning it for Parliament, sent the wrong message about Labour's attitude towards the assembly.

We turned to the 21st Century Party consultation, which Millbank seemed determined to press on with. A week before the NEC, McDonagh had despatched a letter to constituency labour party secretaries informing them that the remit of the 21st

Century Party consultation had been extended to include methods of selection of candidates. This was the way in which my motion, defeated at the previous NEC, had been referred to the 21st Century Party consultation. The deadline for responses was three weeks later, 12 June. I proposed that the deadline should be extended to the end of July, to allow CLP secretaries to call meetings and consult, and that the responses should be put to Conference. Mary Turner seconded me on the extension of the deadline, but not on submission to Conference. McDonagh agreed to extend the deadline to the end of June, which Turner accepted. McDonagh would not contemplate allowing the motions to go to Conference. "We now do things in a consensual rather than a resolutionary way – Liz. We had that debate at Conference and the debate was lost."

There was then a long presentation and even longer discussion on the trials and tribulations of the new membership system and the information technology behind it. The NEC was profoundly unhappy. The system was in chaos. We were constantly reassured that it was being sorted out. Nobody would admit or contemplate that this might be the fault of outsourcing the department. Indeed, the private company was completely exonerated. Everything was blamed on the poor state of the records given by Millbank to the private supplier. The private supplier is SEMA, which was criticised by the House of Commons social services committee for its handling of the Benefits Agency's medical records: "too often [SEMA] fails to deliver an adequate service. . . . At its worst, it puts claimants through examinations which are painful and distressing and gives poor advice." Of course, SEMA was not present at the NEC to take the flak.

Parliamentary selections were taking place. The main interest was in those thirty seats currently held by Labour where the sitting MP was retiring. Only one woman had been selected – NEC member Anne Picking, whom the Chair congratulated. It was noted that there would be fewer women Labour MPs in the next Parliament. We then dived into an on-going row about the National Parliamentary Panel, a newly established list of approved candidates. The rules clearly state that membership of the panel is not a prerequisite for candidates. Christine was seeking selection in Meriden (and was subsequently successful) but was not on the panel. However, in Dundee East, Marilyn Glenn (who was nominated by all the branches in the constituency and had fought the seat for the Scottish Parliament) had been prevented from standing – because she was not on the panel. Mark and I raised this and were told that it was "wrong" but that the selection had been completed and it was too late for Marilyn Glenn. Anne Picking's complaint came from the opposite tack. She said that in her selection contest she was up against "an anti-Anne Picking camp". Her opponent had been rejected by the National Parliamentary Panel and she thought he shouldn't have been allowed to stand against her because this was giving him "two bites at the cherry".

Christine proposed a motion calling on the government to assist the manufacturing sector by reducing the value of sterling, lowering interest rates and publicising its strategy for manufacturing. Job losses at Rover and elsewhere in the manufacturing sector, at a time of general growth, had sent alarm bells through the labour movement. Until very recently, it would have been natural for the Labour NEC to comment on this. But Christine was immediately asked by Vernon Hince if she would refer her motion to the Industry, Culture and Agriculture Policy Commission. She refused: "this is such an important policy decision." The trade unions were very uncomfortable with any vote on this issue at this time. Steve Pickering urged Christine to agree to refer the motion to the policy commission on the grounds that while he supported the sentiment of it, it didn't go far enough. Mike Griffiths adopted a similar argument: "We need a strategic interventionist approach. . . . I'm concerned that the government is not doing all it should do . . . investment, training, productivity levels, R&D . . . but this motion doesn't address the euro." He too wanted the motion referred elsewhere. Dennis Skinner spoke against the motion, particularly on the reference to devaluation: "Playing with the pound and the weak euro isn't the right way." The motion was defeated by thirteen votes to five (Christine, Mark, myself, and the two GMB representatives). The AEEU abstained. UNISON, the TGWU, USDAW, and the GPMU all voted against it – though all officially supported policies similar to those called for in the motion.

We came to the annual discussion on invitations to Conference. Again, Burma, Serbia and the Sudan were to be excluded. Mindful of what had happened last year, I proposed that there should be three other exclusions: the Indonesian ambassador (again); the Pakistan High Commissioner, in light of the military coup; and the Russian ambassador, given the horrific bombardment of Chechnya. Simon Murphy supported me on Pakistan and proposed that Austria also should not be invited (the Haider factor). Clive Soley said that when it came to Indonesia we had to be consistent with the government's foreign policy, that "the democratic process there is continuing" and should be supported. McDonagh agreed not to invite Pakistan or Austria. The vote in favour of inviting the Indonesian ambassador was nine to four (Mark, Christine, Dennis and I) and in favour of inviting the Russian ambassador ten to three (Christine, Dennis and I).

We finally came to an item which had not been mentioned on the agenda, nor was there a written report. It was raised under one of the minutes for the Organisation Sub-committee. Cath Speight, Chair of the Disputes Panel and trade union representative from the AEEU, newly elected in 1999, said that there was a problem with the National Organisation of Labour Students, the Party's student wing. Most of us old hacks round the table were thinking – oh no, not student politics. However, the problem appeared not to be with Labour Students itself, as in the past, but with another case of Millbank interference. Why Millbank should have wanted to interfere in Labour Students (which has a history of providing the shock troops for New Labour, and is firmly under its control) is not something that I ever managed to figure out. Speight said that the election for the Labour Students national executive had been postponed two months earlier as there were complaints over the eligibility of delegates to Labour Students Conference. Having considered the eligibility of various delegates, she was recommending that the election should now proceed by post. That all sounded fair enough. However, Claire

McCarthy (Young Labour representative on the NEC) pointed out that because of an earlier dispute about candidates' eligibility, Speight's recommendation meant that there would be only one candidate on the ballot for Chair of Labour Students (who would therefore be elected unopposed). She proposed that the fair way to proceed was to allow nominations to be reopened before a ballot took place. For some reason, Speight was having none of it. We went to a vote on whether or not the elections were to go ahead, with only one candidate on the ballot for Chair, and that was agreed by seven votes to five (Mark, Christine, Dennis, Claire McCarthy and I). "North Korean style," Mark commented as we voted.

I did an interview for the BBC afterwards and it appeared that Tony Robinson, in his first act as NEC member-elect, had denounced the Labour Students decision and said that nominations should be reopened. It seemed an odd thing for the BBC to care about and I wondered why Robinson had raised it, given his otherwise consistent support for everything Blairite. *Private Eye* later reported that his daughter was the ousted candidate's partner.

The National Policy Forum's single annual vote-taking meeting was coming up again, early in July, and once again the Grassroots Alliance worked to formulate and organise support for minority positions. This year there would be six policy documents to deal with: Education and Employment; Democracy and Citizenship; Economy; Industry, Culture and Agriculture; Environment, Transport and the Regions; and Britain in the World. Not a small task. At least this time around each amendment needed only one proposer and seconder (two delegates rather than nine), but the rule that amendments had to "bubble up" from the submissions remained. And an extra hurdle was added. We were circulated with the draft documents, but (unlike the year before) not with the submissions – from which our amendments had to be drawn. Some local parties and lobbying groups (pensioners, Labour Action for Peace, the World Development Movement) sent copies of their submissions directly to Ann Black and myself. Apart from these, we had to make educated guesses and worked on the assumption that the issues we considered important were likely to have been raised by Party members or, crucially, trade unions.

The trade unions' role at Durham in 1999 had been publicised to trade union activists, and some of their representatives had been given a hard time. A year later, in June, I spoke at a large left fringe meeting at the UNISON conference and explained exactly what had happened at Durham, and how UNISON voted. I was later told that this was quoted back to the UNISON leadership all week and that the faces of Maggie Jones and Anne Picking had been like thunder. The trade union officials, particularly in UNISON, where the left is active and organised, had been reminded that their members were watching. So this year they had a slightly more difficult balancing act – voting with the left and in accordance with their union policy on some issues, whilst simultaneously entering into deals with Millbank to ensure that the relevant amendment (which they officially supported) would not receive the magic thirty-five votes sufficient for it to be debated at Conference.

During the weeks leading up to the July National Policy Forum meeting, I was also active in the campaign to defend asylum seekers, who had been subject to both government and media attack. The meetings were well-attended and passionate. As a member of the Labour NEC, I had a special obligation to make clear my feelings about what was happening. The government's policies of scapegoating asylum seekers, reducing them to penury for having the temerity to claim asylum at all, dispersing them around the country, were barbarous. The gulf between the rhetoric and behaviour of the government and the values of tolerance, diversity and anti-racism held by most Labour Party members was growing wider by the day. The complaint was not that the government was not "the government of our dreams", as Blair put it, or that it was delivering improvements too slowly. The complaint was that on privatisation, welfare benefits, pensions, civil liberties, and especially asylum they were making things worse – implementing destructive policies more akin to Thatcherism than to any form of socialism or social democracy.

I spent very little time at the National Policy Forum, which was held this year in Exeter. In two months I would be completing my stint on the NEC. This would be my last National Policy Forum meeting and one of my last duties as an NEC member. I had been invited to speak to the Marxism 2000 summer school on the Saturday of the National Policy Forum weekend, with Mark Steel and Dave Nellist. The theme was "Where Is Labour Going?" and it was a much more attractive proposition than the National Policy Forum. I saw no point in sitting in workshops, trying to convince delegates who would always do whatever Millbank told them to do. I had, however, ensured that we submitted an amendment on asylum seekers calling for the repeal of the voucher and dispersal systems. Ann and Mark proposed the amendment, and both came under pressure to withdraw it, but refused. Mark told me that he had received a phone call from the Home Office saying that Straw wanted to discuss it with him, but Straw then didn't call. After the Marxism debate, I got on a train down to Exeter and arrived for the Saturday evening so that I could vote the next morning – the only part of the proceedings of any significance.

When I arrived on the Saturday afternoon, the BBC was filming outside. I watched the Party Press Office shepherd two apparently ordinary delegates (actually both on the National Parliamentary Panel) out of the building towards an interview. On the way they briefed them about why the National Policy Forum had been "successful" – and then I watched and listened as the two delegates repeated the brief word for word to the BBC. Once they had finished, I chatted privately to the BBC reporter, a long-standing acquaintance. This appeared to send the Millbank press officer into a mild panic. I last saw him gabbling nervously into his mobile phone.

As usual, there was a "gala dinner" on the Saturday evening, at which the Grassroots Alliance once again stuck to its own table. Prescott was in the middle of the hall, with Roger Lyons, Vernon Hince and other trade union leaders. That week, the press had been full of allegations that Lyons had misused MSF funds. He had denied the allegations, but it seemed extraordinary that he should be swanning around a major Labour Party event quite so sure of himself.

On Sunday morning, Robin Cook was in the chair. There were 140 delegates present, a much better turnout than the year before (the fact that only half the membership of the National Policy Forum had bothered to show up in Durham had received unwelcome publicity). There were also more "unendorsed" amendments – 35 in all – than there had been at Durham, and these were not exclusively proposed by the Grassroots Alliance. After recent events, both the Party leadership and the trade union delegations had become a bit self-conscious about being seen to fix everything behind closed doors. It was convenient for both of them to keep some trade union amendments on the agenda as "unendorsed" so that the relevant union could be seen to be voting for its amendment (rather than withdrawing it) and the Party leadership could be shown to be encouraging debate – while at the same time ensuring that sufficient numbers voted against it to prevent it even going to Conference as a minority position. The leadership had also worked out that the absence of any minority amendments at last year's Conference had discredited the spectacle. So at this year's Conference they were prepared to allow a vote on some, relatively trivial or peripheral, "unendorsed" amendments.

The really contentious motions before the National Policy Forum concerned the gamut of Party members' discontent: privatisation of rail and the underground, Private Finance Initiative and public services, a directly elected House of Lords, the decommissioning of Trident, asylum seekers, increases in progressive taxation and the upper earnings limit for national insurance contributions, increases in the minimum wage, improvements to the Employment Relations Act, prohibiting discrimination on the grounds of sexuality, encouraging comprehensive education, and abolishing charitable status for private schools. There was no way Millbank wanted a conference vote on any of these.

There had been some ducking and diving over asylum seekers. A number of amendments from trade unions had been accepted into the official documents. With the exception of the one from the TGWU (put in Bill Morris's name and no doubt at his insistence), all merely called for a "review" of the system at some unspecified stage. The government could easily live with that. They had, however, been compelled to yield to the TGWU stipulation that the review would use criteria including: an adequate standard of living and security of income for asylum seekers, integration of asylum seekers into communities, maintenance of the dignity of asylum seekers, and measures to help eliminate child poverty. The government didn't like it, but it wasn't a concession that actually cost anything. The government can easily hold a review into the vouchers and decide (even in the teeth of those social criteria) that they are effective. The TGWU policy is that vouchers should be abolished. This amendment could not be guaranteed to achieve that, although it left the door open.

There was also some manoeuvring over electoral reform. The joy of the debate over electoral reform for parliamentary elections is that everybody divides on non-factional sides – although the factional competition between the first-past-the-post and the proportional representation camps is fairly intense. The Grassroots Alliance delegates to the National Policy Forum were divided. Most were passionately in favour of first-past-the-post elections, on the grounds that this system facilitates the election of a Labour government and prevents coalitions. I am pretty agnostic – a position which wins no friends on either side. My priority is accountability: the right of the local electorate to hold their representative to account and the right of the local Labour Party to select and hold accountable the candidate of their choice. For that reason, I am wholly opposed to the list system which entrenches the power of centralised Party machines. Under many forms of proportional representation, it would not have been possible, for example, for the (predominantly Tory) electorate of Tatton to be able to remove their particular Tory MP. However, I also see that justice and diversity demand some kind of proportional adjustment in representation, and I support mechanisms to elect top-up candidates to ensure that the range of political opinions within the electorate is properly reflected. And I agree with the government's policy of holding a referendum on the issue.

Before Exeter, both sides were gearing up for a battle, but by the Sunday morning, the issue on proportional representation had been negotiated away, save for one point. The first-past-the-post campaigners had accepted that the government should hold a referendum, and the one remaining issue was whether, in the run-up to a referendum, the Party would campaign against proportional representation and for maintaining the first-past-the-post system of parliamentary elections.

Christine proposed at the start of the Sunday plenary session the radical suggestion that movers of amendments should have two minutes each to speak to them. Cook was resistant, ostensibly on the grounds that delegates would want to catch the 12.15 train to London (there were trains to London every hour). He went straight to the vote on her proposal (an advance on the previous year) and it was firmly defeated. There would be no speeches in support of the unendorsed amendments, then, but speeches from ministers on each of the six policy documents, followed by six "reports from workshops". Some big shots were there to speak: Blunkett, Straw (apparently none too pleased because he had come to Exeter specifically for the Sunday morning session and, on arrival, was told he had only three minutes for his speech; it later transpired that his driver was stopped for speeding on the way down), Stephen Byers, Secretary of State for Trade and Industry (sitting next to us and laughing nervously when Mark said, "If you're not sure how to vote, Stephen, just follow us"), Prescott, and Cook. The ministers' speeches only dealt with each of the relevant unendorsed amendments; their sole purpose was to explain why they should be opposed (repeating the points already printed adjacent to the unendorsed amendments on the official papers). They usually urged the movers to withdraw, even at this late stage. The reports from the workshops came from the National Policy Forum members of the relevant policy commission – members already committed to the current text of the policy documents and unlikely to support any amendments. They reiterated the message given to the BBC: the process had been harmonious; everyone was happy.

Cook, in the chair, generously waived his right to speak on

Britain in the World. There was only one amendment to be voted on – one we had submitted, at the request of peace movement organisations, calling for the withdrawal of Trident nuclear weapons. Nuclear disarmament is no longer much discussed in the Labour Party, and for the Blairites the very topic has an out-of-date 1980s flavour. Nonetheless, thousands of Party members still believe in unilateral nuclear disarmament and the dismantling of Trident and, with nuclear tests in south Asia raising the stakes yet again, it was clearly an appropriate issue to be discussed at Conference. But only twenty-eight delegates voted for the amendment; Cook did not bother to count the votes against.

Two unendorsed amendments received a majority of votes and were therefore incorporated directly into the policy documents: one to reduce the age at which persons could stand for public office to eighteen (proposed by Young Labour) and another to review the use of standing charges for utility services. Formally, they both represented rejections of the leadership position, but Millbank had already decided to let them through. In addition, seven unendorsed amendments received enough votes to go to Conference as minority positions. Four concerned issues that the leadership could live with (reducing the voting age to sixteen, extending the New Deal grants for school repairs and SureStart programmes for pre-school children into the second term of the Labour government, and imposing higher fines on companies and directors polluting the environment). But there remained three unendorsed amendments to be put to Conference that left the leadership uneasy: the direct election of a majority of the House of Lords, the early introduction of the Advanced Train Protection (ATP) safety system on the railways, and retention of block grants to local education authorities rather than routing funds directly to schools. The last had been pushed by Jeremy Beecham and the local government lobby. I always thought it was unlikely to reach the floor of Conference without a negotiated compromise – and sure enough Beecham withdrew it at Conference. However, at least the local government lobby was prepared to use its muscle at the National Policy Forum; the threat of forcing what New Labour would consider an embarrassing conference debate proved an effective negotiating tool. When Blunkett appealed to Beecham to withdraw the amendment rather than have it put to a vote, Beecham caught my eye and shook his head. Sadly, the trade unions refused to follow a similar course. Their muscle went largely unflexed.

What was most significant were the issues that were voted down, the topics that would not even be aired at Conference. They included Gordon Prentice's amendment that the whole of the second chamber be directly elected, and the Grassroots Alliance amendments on increasing the top rate of tax, abolishing the ceiling on national insurance contributions, increasing welfare benefits, opposition to Private Finance Initiative schemes in schools, homes or hospitals, and support for an annual increase in the level of the minimum wage. John Edmonds was sitting near us. As we watched all of the trade unions vote against our amendment on increasing the minimum wage (there were only nineteen votes in favour), Mark asked Edmonds how he could vote against such an amendment. It was, after all, his own union's policy. Edmonds replied that he had not spent the entire weekend negotiating on the minimum wage to throw away the concessions he had achieved. I have since gone through the Economy policy document and the endorsed amendments, and cannot find anything in them that represents an improvement on the government's original position on the minimum wage. Of the 190 delegates present only seventeen (the Grassroots Alliance) voted against performance-related pay for teachers; only sixteen voted for increased resources for children with dyslexia, and only twenty-eight voted to abolish charitable status for private schools. Only twenty-five voted for discrimination on the grounds of sexuality to be legislated against; the rest were happy with the government's notion that guidelines for employers were sufficient.

We then came to a whole raft of motions proposed by the RMT and by the Grassroots Alliance supporting public ownership of the rail network and of the underground, with particular opposition to the tube being financed by public–private partnership. Despite the fact that they embodied positions held by a majority of Labour Party members and trade unionists and indeed the general public, none of those amendments achieved enough votes to go before Labour's annual conference, even as minority positions. Not even the amendment on public–private partnership for the London tube – the hottest issue in the recent mayoral fiasco – managed it. The core vote of nineteen was the RMT plus the Grassroots Alliance. UNISON – under pressure on this one from its membership – supported amendments for a publicly owned and accountable rail network. But it wasn't enough.

Sadly, the amendment from Ann and Mark criticising the voucher and dispersal elements of the Asylum Act achieved the lowest vote of the session, only fifteen, the core Grassroots Alliance support. All the trade unions, the overwhelming majority of the constituency delegates, the socialist societies and the MPs voted against it.

On electoral reform, Ann and I voted against the amendment calling on the government to promote the first-past-the-post system in any forthcoming referendum. The others from the Grassroots Alliance voted for it. We had enjoyed disagreeing with each other on this issue and we were all smiling as we stuck up our hands to vote. All the amendments on pensions – by common consent a decisive issue in the recent electoral setbacks – had been ruled out of order, on the grounds that pensions had been debated as part of the welfare policy document the previous year. However, we were told that there would be a statement to Conference. There was still no sign of the welfare policy review promised the previous year.

Whenever, during my time on the NEC, I would decide that I had seen all the tricks in Millbank's bag, something new would emerge to amaze me. Two papers were sent out in advance of the July NEC as a result of the 21st Century Party consultation. The first was called "Draft Report on 21st Century Party Consultation on Selections" and the second simply "21st Century Party Consultation". The former paper had emerged from the chaos surrounding our motion to the NEC in March, calling for trade unions to ballot their members in future electoral colleges and for the role of the parliamentarians' vote to be reconsidered. Local parties had been given at most six weeks to submit responses. We were told that submissions had been received from one third of all constituencies and that the trade unions had put in a joint submission, but we were not given copies of any of these submissions. It was therefore impossible to tell whether the document before us on selections reflected the views of the Party or merely those of Millbank.

This document was Millbank's belated attempt to respond to the crisis over the Welsh and London selections. Trade unions were to be required to ballot their members in any future electoral colleges – a victory for us. One member, one vote would be used for the selection of candidates for the European Parliament and also to determine the ranking of candidates on the list – another victory. But Westminster parliamentary selections were to become yet more restrictive: candidates putting their names forward for selection had to be members of the National Parliamentary Panel. Selection panels for local government, the Scottish Parliament, Welsh and London assemblies would remain, thus ensuring that New Labour candidates would predominate and others could be weeded out with minimum fuss. Furthermore, the document explored whole new areas that had not been subject to any consultation. At the back, there was a new section on internal elections. The proposal was that NEC members be elected for two-year terms, rather than annually. Millbank wanted to bring rule changes to October's Conference, so that the two-year term could be implemented as quickly as possible, for the NEC ballot in 2001.

When we arrived at the NEC, a reworked version of the draft was placed in front of us. Over the weekend, there must have some lobbying going on; Millbank had clearly decided that this time it had pushed the boat out too far. The requirement that potential candidates for Westminster selection had to be on the National Parliamentary Panel was deleted. The proposals regarding the NEC elections were still there, but instead of being implemented in 2001, there would be a consultation period with rule changes brought to the 2001 Conference and biennial elections from 2002.

Blair was late to the NEC and so Prescott kicked off. Today's topic was general election preparations. The message was: "we took a lot of stick in the first two years sticking to Tory spending plans" but now new spending will come through. We should be campaigning to win a second term – and a third term. "We have to enthuse Labour Party members. We've put together economic prosperity and social justice." Ian McCartney backed up Prescott: "we have to have a ten-year strategy." The abolition of child poverty, major developments to public services, and dealing with pensioner poverty all depended on a ten-year strategy. I'm sure I wasn't the only one who thought: let's hope the pensioners are still alive to enjoy it in ten years. When Blair arrived, he concentrated on his favourite themes: the press and the Tories. Unusually, the third theme, the perfidy of Party members, was absent. "The press have been giving us a hard time over the last few months." What Blair did not say, but many of us were thinking, was that the press had been giving *him* a hard time over the last few months – the widespread criticism of his suggestion that there should be on-the-spot fines for "hooligans", his son Euan's escapade, leaked emails revealing how preoccupied he was with his public image. "Our opponents' strategy is not to debate policy but to amass cynicism." There was then a long list of the horrors of the Tories: they would limit public spending, make major cuts in social security, exempt employers from the minimum wage; they couldn't increase spending on the NHS because they'd promised tax relief for health insurance; special education would go, and there would be selection in primary schools. "The public comes back to fundamentals, but only if we do so with confidence. We need vision and values – uniting economic prosperity to social justice. This is the first time in Labour Party history that we've had the ability to do that. The Party must be united and campaigning."

Dennis Skinner said that the £43 billion promised in the comprehensive public spending review should be front-loaded as soon as possible so that people could see it, not just in the key seats but also in the heartlands. "We must be able to say we delivered on health and education." The sale of council houses should be kicked into the long grass. Skinner also warned the Prime Minister, "You need to be careful how you carry on in memos. Don't whinge, don't whine." He said that he was opposed to the single currency, and this sparked off some low-key discussion. Claire McCarthy said that the Labour Party believed in the euro if it was in "the best economic interests". Steve Pickering said we needed an informed debate. Hodgson said that we had not been doing as well as we should in selling the message and that Europe was still a problem. Helen Jackson, Michael Cashman and Jeremy Beecham went on about the awfulness of the Tories.

The previous evening, the government had been defeated in the Lords over the repeal of Section 28. Blair did not mention this, but Diana Holland, Diana Jeuda and I all brought it up. Holland said that there was a danger that a positive policy and an inclusive definition of the family were being undermined – I wondered if this was a reference to Blair's leaked emails discussing the importance of "family values". Jeuda said, "There are some things we do because they are right and the abolition of Section 28 is one of them." Michael Cashman took the opposite view: "On Section 28, we should have the courage to say that we are committed to repeal, but we will not put the Local Government Bill at risk." Mary Turner agreed with Skinner on council house sales and asked Blair if a *Sunday Mirror* headline claim that he was taking milk away from schoolchildren was true. For reasons that he did not explain, Clive Soley urged us to remember the 1980s and said that we shouldn't chuck out council house sales.

When Blair replied, he said that the government would not allow the abolition of Section 28 to jeopardise the Local Government Bill. "There's no point in getting defeated again in the Lords" but "we must draw a line and make it clear we haven't given up." He returned to sniping at the press, "We don't have a press that will back us to the hilt as the Tories did in the 1980s. We have the *Guardian*" (grimacing). He put on a fake American accent and told a story of how an American lawyer, at a reception given by Cherie at Downing Street, had said that he thought the

Guardian was "a Tory paper". Mark, Christine and I looked at each other. Then Blair went back to his exhortations. "We're doing the right thing – it takes time to get there. We have to get people back to the record of the government. I don't think we've paid enough attention to explaining what we're trying to do. We've a very clear argument of economic efficiency and social justice. People understand it. It's a chance for everyone to succeed, not just a few at the top. There's a possibility that this is the most successful centre–left government in a hundred years." At this final statement, Clement Attlee, whose portrait dominates NEC meetings, had the grace not to blink.

Prescott backed up Blair and said that we should be "talking it up, not talking it down", while glaring at me. He managed to reassure Mary Turner that the change in funding for school milk was a result of European regulations.

Blair left, and McDonagh introduced the revised paper on selections. She said this was an opportunity to "draw a line" over past arguments about the process. When it came to the proposals for NEC elections, she said that there was long-term continuity of membership in both the trade union and Parliamentary Labour Party sections (the last assertion wasn't true – the PLP section had existed for two years, and only one member – Clive Soley – out of the three originally elected had been re-elected for a second year). In contrast, the constituency section did not have "long-term continuity" and was therefore "more radical, volatile and it changes more frequently. The members never get to grips with the system. That's my observation." Besides, she added, holding the elections only once every two years would save money.

There were howls around the table as McDonagh described the constituency section as "radical and volatile". The NEC, remember, is formally McDonagh's employer; she is supposed to be accountable to it, not the other way around. Besides offending members past and present of the NEC, she had let slip the real reason for the proposed change – the fact that Party members kept voting for the Grassroots Alliance. Christine said that annual elections for the NEC were "a simple question of accountability". Dianne Hayter said that the financial reasons were not the right reasons. Quoting an anonymous member (and thereby distancing herself from the sentiment), she said "annual elections for the NEC are a timely reminder to the leadership of what Labour Party members think". Jeuda said that it was reasonable to consult on the NEC election proposal but she deplored McDonagh's comments. "Whatever you may think of Pete Willsman, you can't say that he didn't get to grips with the NEC in his year of membership. And whatever you think of Christine as a new member, you can't say that she doesn't participate."

Jeremy Beecham said that there should be other options. He wanted to put round the table his own proposal for councillors to be able to participate in electoral colleges selecting a mayoral candidate. The Chair ruled him out of order and said that he could raise those proposals in the consultation. I said that I was delighted to be called "radical and volatile" and quoted the Chartists on annual elections. Prosser came in with the Millbank line: "There should be two-year terms for the NEC because there's no opportunity for individuals to behave in a cohesive fashion. This will be sensitive but all of us should promote the debate in a positive way. Two-year elections mean greater democracy because people come to grips with the organisation." And they would save money: "Finances are more important than two-year elections." Cashman backed her up: "I want the staff to be serving members, not forever having internal elections." Murphy urged the doubters, "Don't throw this out on gut or emotion." Soley went on at some length in support of two-year terms: "The constituency section would be a more effective group. When we had annual elections to the Shadow Cabinet, people were always looking over their shoulder and starting to campaign for the next year."

As Soley was speaking, Mike Griffiths sitting next to me was muttering that Soley's argument was "against accountability" and that he was getting more and more convinced about opposing the proposal as Soley spoke for it. However, Griffiths was the next to be called – and spoke in favour of two-year elections, saying, "The constituency section is weak because there is no continuity." Hodgson weighed in as well, urging us not to vote against a "consultation" document: "It's bigoted to say that you can't

consult because there are certain aspects you disagree with."
Hodgson, like everyone else in the room, knew perfectly well that
a Millbank-led "consultation" was not about listening to Party
members, but selling something to them.

McDonagh replied, somewhat defensively. "I wasn't saying that
the individuals are stupid, but that the group as a whole is weak."
She then concentrated on the financial savings. Because she had
said that the document was merely going out to consultation, no
vote was taken on it.

We then came to the second paper and the meat of the 21st
Century Party consultation. Would the NEC abolish the general
committees of local Labour parties or not? Millbank's sales pitch
had not been particularly effective with the membership on this
one, no doubt partly as a result of the discontent of Party
members over the London selection. We were not shown the
submissions, but the document as a whole backed away from
recommending the abolition of general committees – yet. The
document recommended a further review of the organisation of
constituency Labour parties. This review should consider both
giving the executive of the constituency Labour party more tasks,
and removing political debate (and above all, votes) from the
general committee. There could be little doubt that the vast bulk
of the submissions to Millbank had opposed the abolition of
general committees and that in the wake of the election results
members' inflamed sensitivities had forced Millbank to delay. The
plan now was to bore Party members to death with endless reviews
of organisation, thus preventing Party members from discussing
and voting on policy (Millbank's real aim) and grinding them
into submission on the abolition of the general committees.

Millbank argued that there was "a huge desire for change", and
that individual members wanted lively political discussions, interesting meetings, campaigning and "to be valued", but not necessarily to have votes. The branch structure should be retained but
(as far as general committees were concerned) there should be
"a co-ordinating body for Westminster CLPs". There was to be a
three-phase process to achieve this: review of all constituency
Labour parties and branches; implementation of new campaign

and development plans; and evaluation and future feedback to the NEC. This was not to start until after the general election but there would be pilot projects "preferably in moribund CLPs". This was all nodded through. Again, we were deprived of a vote.

The only media report of this NEC meeting appeared in *The Times*, headlined "NEC in revolt over new vote rule". Presumably Millbank did not feel comfortable spinning to the *Guardian*, given Blair's unscripted jibe.

Taking Leave of Wonderland

As I prepared for my last National Executive Committee meeting in September, a blessed sense of relief came over me. Dealing with the meetings had grown slightly easier over the two years. At first, the hostility towards us from everyone else in the room had been so strong you could almost feel it physically. As the months went on, that receded. Some members of the NEC relaxed enough with us to exchange pleasantries or jokes. Others remained deeply suspicious, but they mainly just kept their distance. However, the dissipation of the personal hatred did not affect the political stakes. Everyone in the room at the NEC meetings – some fifty or so people, including members of the NEC and Labour Party staff – was watching us. If we made any sort of mistake – if we failed to spot a detail in a laid-round paper, if we expressed ourselves poorly – it would be used against us. Looking back over the two years, I am astonished to find how much of the NEC's time was taken up with efforts to stifle or silence our small rump of dissidents. Again and again, we were forced to sit there listening to everyone else attack us – some kind of ritual humiliation that we were required to endure as the price of having won the elections. At least Vernon Hince had not continued Brenda Etchells's habit of reading a coded little homily against us from the chair at the start of each meeting.

When you are in such a small minority in a meeting, the pressure to keep quiet and not to object is immense, especially when your previous objections have been repeatedly slapped down and you've been told that you object too much. It feels ridiculous sometimes to object to what seems a small detail –

which may range from some dubious wording in a document to the invitation to the Indonesian ambassador to attend the Party's annual conference. You know that the fate of your objection will not be decided on its merits, and that whatever arguments you make, the decision will be taken by Millbank according to its own unique brand of logic. So you ask yourself, can I be bothered to raise this just so that it can be shot down? And you wish for a quiet life. Then you remember the price of keeping quiet, of passively accepting what you know to be wrong – and you remember that a lot of people voted for you, and that their claims come first. If you allow yourself to be silenced by the hostility of others or by your own sense of futility, you've taken the first step to being incorporated, and after a few more steps you're part of the problem, not the solution. So I would remind myself that what mattered was how Party members perceived our actions, not how other members of the NEC perceived them. When it felt as though we were just going through the motions, we were in fact putting down necessary democratic markers, registering views that often represented the majority of Party members, and significant sections of the general public. And I'm glad we did it. We provided some small measure of representation to people and ideas that go largely unrepresented, not just in New Labour, but in our society in general.

So I had no regrets about my two years, but none either about my imminent departure. There comes a point at which it is impossible to engage with such a cult-like atmosphere. Like Lewis Carroll's Humpty Dumpty, New Labour believed "when I use a word . . . it means just what I choose it to mean". At the NEC, cabinet members or Millbank staff would repeat the most implausible versions or explanations of events (the *Guardian* was a Tory paper, the election result was a disaster for Livingstone, rules existed even though no one had written them down) and nearly everyone around the table would nod in agreement. When senior Party figures moaned about the *Guardian* and *Newsnight*, nobody seemed to consider how independent media in a democratic country should behave towards a government. At meeting after meeting, we were attacked for reporting events at the NEC in

Tribune or *Labour Left Briefing*, whilst Millbank freely fed its own spin on the meetings direct to the mass media, grossly misrepresenting discussions and decisions and especially anything said or done by the Grassroots Alliance. NEC members reverentially accepted McDonagh's constant assertions that she was not responsible for press reports – when everyone around the table knew that only Millbank could have been the source of the reports.

And of course whenever something went wrong it was anybody's fault but Millbank's. The unpopularity of any government measures could only be the result of a lapse in presentation or a conspiracy. If people didn't vote Labour, that was blamed on Labour Party members or on Labour Party councillors. The complete meltdown of the membership department after it had been outsourced had nothing to do with the decision to outsource. Listening to NEC members reassuring each other that two plus two equalled five was like walking into wonderland. Readers will have noticed that most NEC members did not even bother to put the line – a few would engage in limited debate with the Grassroots Alliance to defend Millbank's position, but the majority would say not a word, contenting themselves with sticking their hands up at Millbank's command.

The reason for the NEC's addiction to double-speak is political. New Labour's agenda for the Labour Party is to disenfranchise the membership, to winnow out independent-minded candidates (MPs, MEPs, councillors, etcetera) and to centralise power. The policy agenda is to tilt away from universal welfare benefits towards means-testing, to privatise public services, to reduce civil liberties, and to preserve the current tax status of the rich. Of course, Blair cannot say this in so many words to the NEC, not least because of the discomfort it would bring to the very large trade union presence at the meetings.

The trade union representatives were the only people at the meetings with a real chance to challenge New Labour's agenda, and they could have made a difference had they wanted to. Mary Turner made her points about public sector work, Derek Hodgson bristled over Post Office privatisation, Diana Holland raised employment rights and gender issues. Although their muted criticism rarely translated into votes or any follow-up action, their interventions were uncomfortable for Millbank. None of the other trade union representatives uttered so much as a whisper of protest at privatisation, cuts to public sector workers, the low level of the minimum wage, or the government's pensions policy. Yet nearly all of them represent unions opposed to privatisation, and in favour of an index-linked minimum wage and restoring the link between pensions and earnings. Their bargain with Millbank seemed to be that, provided Blair, Prescott and the others argued the government's case in a language of social justice, they would not press union policies at the NEC. For them, as for many others in New Labour, the height of political sophistication consists of saying what you don't believe and voting for what you don't believe in order to maintain some unquantifiable and virtually indiscernible "influence" over a leadership that holds you in contempt.

I headed to the September meeting of the NEC determined to make the most of my last chance to question Tony Blair. I had decided to ask how a Labour prime minister could justify the increase in the gap between rich and poor revealed in recent academic studies. Mark and I had also put down a motion saying that the Party should drop the use of "New Labour" and we hoped to have some fun with it. I wondered what sort of mood Blair would be in – he had been taken on the hop by the fuel protesters and was facing opinion polls that showed Labour and the Tories neck and neck for the first time since 1992. Frustratingly, it was a nightmare public transport morning (roadworks in Hackney, the closure of King's Cross, etcetera) and I arrived at the NEC forty-five minutes late. As I walked in, Blair was absent and Prescott was already replying to questions, saying: "We will communicate what you said about pensions." (I later learned from Mark and Christine that there had been a general if belated agreement that the 75p increase in pensions had not been a success.)

Prescott then made a reference to "all these books being written". Since I had spent the previous month putting together the first draft of this book, I looked up in alarm, but he was glaring at Mo Mowlam (whose biography was published a week

later), Prescott stressed the propaganda purpose of Conference
(to be held the following week). "We've got to make sure we get
our Conference right. The fuel business will dominate. . . . We say
we're listening. There are more people in work than ever before.
Values are the difference between us and the Tories. The Tories
have reinforced that argument. We have a strong economy and
we're meeting the priorities of people in public services. Arro-
gance is the last thing in Tony Blair [I wonder whether Prescott
really believes that]. But they've been able to stick it to him. We
need Conference to get our values across. We will not be dictated
to by people on a picket line. If we had given in at the beginning,
like the French did, odium would have been dumped on us." This
was said by the former NUS shop steward denounced by Harold
Wilson when he led the national seamen's strike as part of a
"tightly knit group of politically motivated men". Some of the
NEC broke into applause.

Most of the NEC's business was taken up with arrangements for
Conference. Two senior officers from the Brighton police
attended to talk about security. There was much discussion of the
various demonstrations expected outside Conference: the
Countryside Alliance, fuel protesters and anti-globalisation protesters. The police were clear about their duties: "we must facilitate anyone making lawful protests . . . we will try to keep the
balance of impartiality to all sides". Some members of the NEC
seemed unhappy with this, and wanted the police to take a harder
line.

We then moved on to deal with three constitutional amendments that would have gone some way towards reinstating democratic debate at Conference. One would have allowed the
constituencies to hold their own ballot on prioritising "contemporary motions" (at present that power lies effectively with the
trade unions). Another would have allowed motions to be submitted on topics not covered in the National Policy Forum reports.
And the third, most radically, would have allowed amendments to
the reports. This came from the Socialist Education Association.
Dianne Hayter said that the SEA was feeling particularly squeezed
out. But although she was the socialist societies representative on

the NEC, she did not advocate acceptance of the SEA motion, but merely that it be considered "at such a time as we consider improvements to the National Policy Forum". Millbank's line of argument was defensive and technical; all these amendments had to be opposed, we were told, because they would tie the hands of the Conference Arrangements Committee. The NEC voted to reject all the amendments. Only four of us – Christine, Mark, Dennis and I – voted in the minority. Dianne Hayter abstained.

Diana Jeuda complained that Millbank had interfered in the debate over the composition of the House of Lords in the Democracy and Citizenship Policy report. It was proposed that Conference should vote on a single minority amendment – calling for the majority of the second chamber to be elected, rather than appointed (Blair's position). We called the minority amendment "the campaign for a slightly democratic House of Lords" since the amendment proposing a wholly elected second chamber had been voted down at the NPF. Jeuda complained that Mo Mowlam (who had left the meeting by then) had sent out a letter to conference delegates urging them to vote against the amendment, and in favour of the policy document position, without the same opportunity being given to the supporters of the amendment. Mark added that he had seen Mowlam's letter, and it was on Labour Party headed paper. McDonagh said that she did not know anything about the matter, but would look into it. If a letter had gone out, another letter with the alternative position would be circulated. As far as I know, it never was.

During what appeared to be a routine item as to who would chair which section of Conference, Vernon Hince said grumpily from the chair, "I'm disappointed that the Chair of the Party [Hince himself] is not chairing the final session of Conference." The final session of Conference was to be addressed by Nelson Mandela, and Michael Cashman had been pencilled in by Millbank to chair. Jeuda looked up, surprised: "You mean that wasn't your choice?" she said to Hince. "The Chair of the Party should have first choice of which sessions to chair." Millbank officials shifted in their seats. The matter was not pursued further at the meeting – but in the end Hince got to chair that final session.

Tony Benn was standing down as MP in Chesterfield, and Millbank was meddling in the selection of his successor. Helen Seaford, who had received six local nominations, had not been shortlisted by the NEC by-election panel, which had preferred several other candidates who had received fewer nominations but had been shortlisted. One of these was Liz Kendall, Harriet Harman's researcher, who was rumoured to be New Labour's favoured candidate (but eventually lost to local candidate and former MP Reg Race). Mark, Christine and Dennis Skinner all complained about the injustice done to Seaford. It emerged that the by-election panel had consisted of only two people: Clive Soley owned up to being one; the other name was not mentioned but turned out to be Sally Powell (who sat in silence during the discussion). Soley said that the panel members were "acutely aware" of the number of nominations each candidate had – without explaining why they had refused to shortlist a leading and local contender. Six of us voted against the recommended short-list: Mark, Christine, Dennis, Mary Turner, Steve Pickering and I. Thirteen voted in favour.

Finally, we came to our motion about "New Labour". It confirmed that the Party's official title remained "The Labour Party", and proposed that all references to "New Labour" on stationery, publicity, membership cards and by spokespersons be removed; it also rededicated the NEC itself and the Labour Party to fight for the values of social justice, democracy, equality and the redistribution of power and wealth, in order to ensure victory at the next general election. It had been Mark's idea; we had written it together. Mark described it to the NEC as "a leaving present" from him and me, and referred to Philip Gould's (Blair's adviser and focus group analyst) description of the New Labour brand as "past its sell-by date". I said that "New Labour" had become synonymous in the eyes of Party members and the public with control-freakery and spin-doctoring, with arrogant incompetence and with the Dome. We waited for a chorus of outraged rebuttals. Instead, Margaret Wall moved that we go straight to a vote. Twelve voted to terminate debate there and then, with seven against (the four of us, plus Beecham, Helen Jackson and Jeuda). The motion itself was defeated by five votes (us four – and Jeuda, finally!) to fourteen.

I left, with a sense of liberation.

Conference was held the following week in Brighton. This year, two hundred constituency parties – about one third of the total – had not bothered to send delegates. Some saw no point to the exercise, some could not find anyone willing to go, and some could not afford to send anyone.

In recent years, as I have recounted above, Conference has changed beyond all recognition. Nowadays its proceedings are of so little significance that the hall is half-empty, even for ministerial set-pieces. Both the media and the delegates know that the real action is elsewhere, and they behave accordingly. And the delegates themselves have changed. It is rare to see anyone who is not dressed to the nines, often at some expense. In the past, delegates of all political shades were argumentative and opinionated; these days they walk around in mute awe of ministers and officials. Many seemed flushed with excitement at being cast in a non-speaking walk-on part in the New Labour spectacle.

All the activity now takes place in the coffee bars, and at the evening receptions. I do not attend corporate-sponsored receptions, so I have no idea what goes on there. From reports, various senior ministers appear and do the rounds. Delegates jostle to have the opportunity to speak to, or better still be photographed with, a minister. Some of the senior ministers elicit a popstar-like response: there are reports of women delegates undoing the top button on their blouses as Blair circulates at a reception.

Unlike the previous two years, the press (with the honourable exception of Matthew Parris) paid very little attention to the corporate logos festooned around Conference. The £300,000 bridge (paid for by UNISON) between the conference hotel and the conference centre, allowing senior politicians to glide unmolested over the unwashed multitude, did attract some criticism. But overall the media, like the Labour left, has become so used to New Labour's links with big business that it has lost its sense of outrage.

The debate over pensions, however, brought Conference briefly to life, and recalled both the good and the bad of the old days. The vote against the platform was Blair's first defeat at Conference since 1994 – and could have been avoided if New Labour was less committed to control-freakery. The saga had started back at the Durham National Policy Forum in 1999, when the trade unions had abandoned their support for restoring the link between pensions and earnings in return for a national debate on welfare. That debate never took place. At the Exeter National Policy Forum in July 2000, motions on restoring the link with earnings were ruled out of order, some said at the insistence of Gordon Brown. A number of unions had faced the wrath of their members after their votes the previous year, and had been anxious to redeem themselves. When the amendment had been ruled out at the Exeter meeting, Darling had been forced by trade union discontent to concede that there would be a special statement on pensions to Conference.

The Economic Policy Commission met on 21 September (the week before Conference) and approved a statement prepared by Brown arguing against the restoration of the earnings link. UNISON and the GMB were so incensed that they submitted contemporary resolutions on pensions to Conference, as did ten constituency parties. Conference Arrangements Committee, aware that UNISON and the GMB were amongst the heaviest hitters in the trade union section, decided not to confront them and ruled that the resolutions were in order. Whether or not they really fell within the definition of contemporary resolutions was a matter for dispute. But the political reality was that the motions had to be taken, showing that the notion of "contemporary resolutions" was really a convenient fiction. UNISON, the GMB, and the TGWU block votes ensured that pensions topped the priorities ballot and guaranteed that the issue would be debated.

On the Tuesday of Conference things began to get interesting. Apparently, Rodney Bickerstaffe was coming under sustained pressure from ministers to remit UNISON's resolution, that is, to withdraw it without a vote. Formally, it would then be considered by the NEC or the National Policy Forum. In fact, it would die. He was said to have been kept up until 1am by Brown and

Prescott. He refused to remit. The NEC met at 7.30am on Wednesday morning (I was not staying in Brighton and had not been told about the meeting, so was not present). The meeting lasted only fifteen minutes. NEC members were told that UNISON and the GMB were "reconsidering their position" and that their composited resolution would be withdrawn. Copies of the composited resolution were then removed from members of the NEC. The constituencies supporting the composited resolution were told the same thing. It transpired later that UNISON and the GMB had not agreed to withdraw, but only to look at an alternative wording proposed by Brown, which in the end proved unacceptable to them.

Constituency delegates supporting the UNISON composite were called to what was described as a "re-compositing" meeting, which was actually a meeting to put pressure on them to remit. They walked in to find Gordon Brown, Alistair Darling and Ian McCartney – but no one from UNISON or the GMB. The ministers tried to persuade the delegates to remit – because, despite all the pressure, Bickerstaffe was still refusing to do so.

The NEC met again over lunch on Wednesday. The pensions debate was scheduled for that afternoon. Again, I was not present, having not been told about the meeting (even though I was in Brighton, speaking at a fringe meeting). The NEC meeting went on and on. Margaret Wall had to leave to chair the next conference session, which was starting. Various luminaries were rounded up to sit on the conference platform, so that no one would notice that the NEC was elsewhere. At 3pm (an hour after Conference had started), the NEC voted, by eighteen votes to eight, that if the resolution was not remitted, it would recommend a vote against it. The eight were: Christine, Mark, Dennis Skinner, Anne Picking and Maggie Jones (usually loyal Blairites, but this time compelled to back their own union, UNISON), Mary Turner, Steve Pickering, and Diana Holland – the Grassroots Alliance plus UNISON, the GMB, and the TGWU.

I arrived in Conference about 3pm, to find the NEC trickling back from its emergency meeting. For once the hall was packed, and there was an air of expectancy. Suddenly, Margaret Wall announced that Conference would move now to an unscheduled question-and-answer session with Alistair Darling, chaired by Michael Cashman. Attention switched away from the platform to Darling and Cashman seated casually next to a low coffee table. They were trying to look relaxed and informal. Darling made a speech defending the government's position on pensions. Then various delegates were called by Cashman to put questions to Darling. Out of the fourteen he called, only two voiced any criticism of the government's policy. Of the two critical questioners, one of them (Tony West of ASLEF) had the microphone switched off halfway through his question. The other twelve between them managed to highlight all the arguments the government wanted highlighted, and Darling was given a free run.

Finally, at 5pm, we came to the debate. Bickerstaffe moved the composite and my friend Sarah Cotterill from Manchester Central seconded it. John Edmonds made a point of speaking in support – and even used the dreaded word "tax". Diana Holland also spoke in support. A number of compromises had already been agreed. The motion called for an "immediate and substantial" rise in the state pension, but the link with earnings had been rendered ambiguous by the insertion of the words "for example" before the reference to the link. Despite that compromise, New Labour pulled out all the stops to prevent a debate. Some of us felt that it was a problem of New Labour's own making. Had they not ruled motions on pensions out of order at the National Policy Forum, any debate at Conference would have been far more manageable.

During the debate, Millbank people and UNISON officials had been scurrying backwards and forwards between the platform and the UNISON delegation. From the NEC seats at the front of the hall, we had a direct view of the show. It appeared that even members of the UNISON delegation were putting pressure on Bickerstaffe to remit. He kept shaking his head. When he was finally asked out loud by the platform whether he would remit, he refused. For Rodney Bickerstaffe, on the verge of retirement, this gesture of defiance had been a long time coming.

There was a card vote – unusual in today's Labour Party – and the result was announced later that evening. The government had been defeated by 60.2 per cent to 39.8 per cent. Three and a half years into the Labour government, and after three successive conferences of near-total acquiescence, the trade unions had sent a message to 10 Downing Street. But, in a distressing change from the past, they had done so without the support of the constituencies. Trade unions had voted for UNISON's motion by 84 per cent to 16 per cent. In contrast, constituency delegates had voted against the motion by 64 per cent to 36 per cent. That role reversal would have been inconceivable only a few years before. In any case, even before the vote was taken, Blair and Brown had announced to the media that they would not alter government policy, whatever the conference decided.

The following day, Millbank successfully headed off the other scheduled conference revolt. "Immigration and asylum" had come second in the priorities ballot, thanks to the TGWU, which had submitted a motion expressing opposition to the voucher scheme. An identical motion had been passed unanimously by the TUC three weeks earlier. Regrettably, the TGWU agreed to remit the motion after Straw said that he would "reconsider" the prohibition on asylum seekers receiving change from supermarkets when they shop with vouchers. The *Independent*'s editorial the following day said: "Bill Morris has conceded too cheaply on the question of vouchers for asylum seekers." I assume that Morris was told that the leadership had already suffered one defeat that week, on pensions, and couldn't afford another. For the sake of what Millbank defines as Party unity, and for an insignificant concession (in comparison with the iniquity of the voucher scheme), the TGWU left asylum seekers out in the cold. Conference reverted to its trade fair atmosphere. I noticed that Delyth Morgan, one of Millbank's candidates for the NEC, was given the opportunity to speak from the platform (in her professional capacity with the Breakthrough Breast Cancer charity) and a slot in the Conference newsletter.

I went back to London on the train, happy to miss my very last opportunity to attend the NEC. It would be the annual ritual, with both the old and the new members present. I hoped I had avoided the indignity of being officially thanked by Blair for my work on the NEC, but three weeks later, a framed certificate arrived in the post. It was "in recognition of service on the NEC" and was signed by Tony Blair and Margaret McDonagh. It was accompanied by a formal thank-you letter from McDonagh – the only letter I received from her (besides notices of meetings and documents) during my two years on the NEC. I've not yet decided what to do with the certificate.

Afterword: The Future

Having completed my duties on the National Executive Committee, I contemplated my position as a Labour Party member.

My reasons for political activity remained the same as when I joined the Party at the age of sixteen. I want to be part of a movement that changes the world for the better, that reduces the inequalities between rich and poor, that works to end poverty and war, and to build a common human home where every individual has the right to a decent standard of living, to health care, education and democratic freedoms. When I joined the Labour Party, I saw working within the Party to bring about those goals as part of a broader movement. As far as I was concerned, campaigning on single issues went hand in hand with Labour Party activism.

I always saw myself as a practical political activist, pursuing practical ends. In 1993, while I was a councillor in Islington, the Labour Council decided to close two nurseries in order to save money. There was a large local protest against this unpopular measure. At the council meeting that took the decision, nine Labour councillors (including myself) broke the Labour whip in order to vote against the closures, and the public gallery was packed with protesters. Once the decision had been made, parents and staff occupied the two nurseries in protest. They campaigned on the streets, petitioning, writing letters to the local press, obtaining some television coverage. They kept one of the occupations going for six months. And they were supported by local Labour Party members, who helped with the campaign, invited the parents to speak to Labour Party branch meetings, and moved motions in their support. I was one of the Labour

Party supporters (and also helped with the occupation). After six months, and a great deal of hard campaigning, the Labour Party in Islington called for the cut to be reversed and the remaining nursery to be reopened. The majority of Labour councillors did not agree with this, but were sensitive to electoral pressure and to pressure from Party members; they reopened the nursery. The occupation and the campaign had consumed many months in the lives of a number of parents, staff and their supporters. But we were successful. Achieving that sort of result in today's New Labour Party would be nigh on impossible.

New Labour is qualitatively different from the old broad alliance that used to make up the Labour Party. The argument within the labour movement used to be over how effectively, and at what speed, the Labour government was taking steps to ameliorate the worst excesses of capitalism. It was taken for granted that there should be some progress towards greater equality and redistribution. That is no longer the case. For New Labour, global capitalism is liberating and progressive. In so far as the Labour government of 1997–2001 took any measures to ameliorate or restrain global capitalism – the minimum wage, employment rights – it did so as a result of residual commitments forced on it by the labour movement in the past. In office, New Labour watered down both these measures, and more than compensated its friends in big business by reducing corporate taxes overall and pushing ahead with privatisation. In its next term, it will be saddled with even fewer promises to the movement. This is Millbank's great success, and the reason why so much energy was expended on keeping that largely powerless body the NEC in line.

It does not do to sound too nostalgic about previous Labour governments. Their records were mixed, although the creation of the welfare state was a monumental achievement. In foreign policy, New Labour has shown itself no different to previous Labour governments, offering Washington uncritical support, selling arms, dealing with tyrants. But no other Labour government has presided over an increase in the gap between rich and poor. No other Labour government has shown itself to be so punitive towards benefit claimants. No other Labour government has reduced, rather than extended, the parameters of the welfare state. No other Labour government has excluded some of the poorest groups from sharing in the rising economic prosperity of the rest of the country. And no other Labour government has made such efforts to roll back our civil liberties.

New Labour is Thatcher's legacy to the Labour Party and her ultimate triumph. She refashioned the opposition in her own image and ideology. Her view that there was no alternative has prevailed within the Labour Party. If there were a hope of ridding Labour of New Labour, there would be a political reason for remaining in the Party. But the chances of reclaiming the Party for the old broad alliance seem to me to be minuscule.

Party membership and activity have declined. No young person filled with ideals and enthusiasm would consider joining today's Labour Party. The Party is quite simply not rejuvenating itself, except with a small clique of young people for whom politics is merely a career option. Long-standing members are leaving the Party or drifting into inactivity as a result of disgust at New Labour policies and frustration at the Party's control-freakery. Increasingly, Party meetings, in London at least, are dominated by members of the managerial elite, who believe that society is best run from the top down, by highly paid experts (that is, people like themselves).

During my two years on the NEC, I attended and spoke at more than one hundred Party meetings up and down the country. Every meeting was a little smaller, a little more demoralised, than the last. I was asked over and over again what justification there was for staying in the Party, including by members who a few years ago would have considered themselves well to my right.

The Party's decision-making structures have been changed to such an extent that the opportunity to influence Party policy has almost disappeared. Again, one should avoid nostalgia. The old system was unwieldy, subject to backdoor manipulation. But at least there was the opportunity for local parties and trade unions to put motions directly to Conference, have them printed on the agenda, debated and maybe even passed. Formally, the system of policy making was straightforward, relatively public and transparent, even if in practice it was subject to deal-making. Under the new system, the process is managed, start to finish, from the top down. It incorporates all the worst excesses of the previous system, and then adds some more.

The battle over Party members' right to select their own candidates for public office has enjoyed a high profile and remains Millbank's priority. In 1995, I was one of the first of New Labour's casualties and since then, its ability to control candidate selection has become far more institutionalised. Candidates for every public office except Westminster must now be drawn only from authorised, vetted lists. Westminster candidates not on the approved list must be interviewed by the NEC. Occasionally, a sufficiently high-profile candidate cannot be weeded out by a selection panel – Rhodri Morgan or Ken Livingstone. Where that is the case, Millbank gerrymanders the electoral system. Whilst both Morgan and Livingstone have had their revenge, that has come about as a result of events outside the Party – Livingstone elected as an independent, the Welsh Assembly's vote of no confidence in Alun Michael. Around the country, Labour's public representatives are overwhelmingly those preferred by Millbank, and the innumerable Party members excluded from the system are left impotent and unrepresented.

All this has profoundly hampered the Labour left. Over the last fifteen years, the image of the Labour left has changed significantly. During the 1980s, we were portrayed as manipulative, bedsit conspirators seeking to subvert the Labour Party and civilisation as we know it. Nowadays, we are principally seen as victims, losers. Neither image reflects reality. In my experience, the Labour left was comprised of thoughtful, idealistic people active in their own communities. They wanted to help build a socialist society, and saw the Labour Party as a pragmatic means to that end. The Labour left has also always been part of a wider progressive movement including the trade unions, environmental activists, peace groups, women's, gay and anti-racist campaigns and so on. Contrary to its popular image, I do not think that the Labour left was old-fashioned, or bogged down in defending practices that went out with the dinosaurs. It was a creative, diverse and democratic force. Of course, it doesn't do to sound too sentimental – the left has had its share of sectarianism and difficult people over the years. But today the progressive, idealistic people who brought energy and ideas to the Labour Party have mostly torn up their Party cards, and they have not been replaced.

The ascendancy of New Labour within the Party has meant a narrowing of the Labour left's horizons. Where once it was trying to achieve substantive changes in Party or even government policy, now it is delighted if a candidate is allowed on to a shortlist or if a motion is not ruled out of order. At election times, it finds itself handing out leaflets and knocking on doors for candidates who did not win in a fair contest and promoting policies many Party members find downright offensive. Certainly, all Party members have made compromises in their Party activity. Compromises are a necessary part of political life. No Party member could ever expect to agree with 100 per cent of the contents of all the leaflets they have handed out. But there comes a point when handing out leaflets promoting vouchers for asylum seekers, tax breaks for big business, or restrictions on civil liberties cannot be justified, especially when the supposed justification rests on the unlikely chance of changing Labour Party policy at some unspecified future time.

The pressure from New Labour is such that the Labour left these days rarely speaks its mind in public. Too often we are reduced either to talking in code or to muttering in private. There comes a point at which the talk is so coded, so riddled with defensive caveats, that the core message is lost. There also comes a point at which the degree of censorship administered by New Labour becomes self-policing, instinctive. When the secret policemen can control your words or actions without the need to issue threats, they have won.

The Labour left is diminishing in size; its expectations are at an all-time low; it is required to promote policies and candidates at election time profoundly at variance with its principles. Some individuals solve the last dilemma by abstaining from election activity, or ducking and diving. In the long term, that is not a sustainable strategy – not for those of us who believe the franchise is a precious achievement, an indispensable democratic lever.

Tony Benn has highlighted the "crisis of representation" caused by the transformation of the Labour Party. My experience in the Labour Party, and in particular my two years on the NEC, has led me to believe that this crisis cannot be addressed effectively from within the Labour Party. The establishment consensus, reflected in the big business underpinning of all the major parties, has to be challenged on a much wider front. Too many vulnerable people, too many vital ideas, are being left out of the public debate.

An alternative "counter-conference" challenging the New Labour big business agenda had been organised to coincide with the first day of Labour's 2000 Conference. Called "Our World is Not for Sale", it was part of the anti-corporate, anti-globalisation movement that hit the headlines in 1999 with the protests in Seattle against the World Bank. The counter-conference was held in Hove Town Hall, just down the road from Labour's conference centre in Brighton. I spent the day there, rather than at the "official" conference. However, at the last minute, it seemed that the counter-conference would be stopped in its tracks. Even though the Town Hall had been booked months in advance, senior officials in the New Labour-controlled Brighton and Hove Council had tried to cancel the booking, allegedly on commercial grounds. It seemed they feared this particular booking might somehow compromise other bookings of local facilities made that week by the Labour Party. Along with several others, I protested to Brighton and Hove Council. After the local newspaper ran an indignant editorial on the council's manoeuvre and the right of free speech, it backed down, and the counter-conference proceeded. Several of the organisers of the counter-conference, who had never been members of the Labour Party, were shocked at the flagrantly partisan attempt to withhold public facilities from a legitimate public event. Those of us who were, or had been, in the Labour Party, and were used to the factional proclivities of New Labour, were less surprised.

The counter-conference was a roaring success. It was attended by an overspill audience of more than a thousand (mainly young) people and was addressed by George Monbiot (the environmental and anti-corporate writer and campaigner), Susan George (authoritative critic of the World Bank, the World Trade Organisation and other transnational institutions), Tony Benn MP, Mark Thomas, Jeremy Corbyn MP, Mark Seddon and Alan Simpson MP. Here was a crowd of people who really did want to change the world, and were prepared to get down to serious discussion about how to do it. They were enthusiastic and, despite discussing the horrors of globalisation, optimistic that a better world could be achieved. Chairing the final session, I read out to the counter-conference details of three fringe meetings at the "official" conference up the road. As I read out the names of the corporate sponsors, and the titles of the meetings they were organising, the audience gasped in amazed outrage at the flagrant nature of the tie-up between big business and government. That evening, I made the same points to a Labour left fringe meeting, attended by some of the stalwarts of the Labour left, all socialists and all committed to achieving a better world. There was no reaction. Despite their opposition to New Labour's links with big business, they have spent so many years watching New Labour close up that they have lost their capacity to be shocked by it.

Being a member of the Labour Party is not, of course, a bar to other political activity, such as participating in the struggle against corporate globalisation. The counter-conference did not exclude Labour left-wingers; indeed several of the speakers were well-known Labour left MPs or activists. But events inside the Labour Party were seen as irrelevant to the success or failure of the democratic challenge to the multi-national corporations.

For the whole of my adult life, I have believed that, whatever the faults of the Labour Party, it was an essential part of the movement for social change, and that a Labour government, whatever its faults, would help to bring about positive social change and to reduce the gap between rich and poor. My membership of the Labour Party was not a lifestyle choice; it was part (and a major part) of my commitment to achieving a better world. Now that New Labour has taken over the Labour Party, and the New Labour government appears to be intent on making the world safe for deregulated capitalism, I cannot see how membership of the Labour Party can be part of bringing about positive social change. The only justification for retaining membership, as a socialist, is if there is a real prospect of reversing the grip New Labour has over the Party. As I believe my account of my two years' membership of the NEC makes clear, New Labour has so effectively robbed the Party of its democratic structures – and so effectively manipulated what remains – that there is no longer any realistic prospect of such a reversal.

I now live in Hackney, one of the poorest boroughs in the country, governed by a Labour–Tory coalition. The council is in deep financial crisis, proposing to cut over one quarter of its budget and privatise most of its services, even though Hackney's housing benefit service has ground to a halt since it was privatised. Community groups and trade unions are campaigning against the cuts and privatisation, urging the council to lobby the government to obtain more resources. Not one Labour councillor will even speak to them. In fact Labour councillors in Hackney now spend far more time and energy attacking the community groups and trade unions than they spend pressing the Labour government to deal fairly with Hackney. An attempt by the remnant of the Labour left to raise the issues in the local Party failed miserably when the left was easily outnumbered by the massed ranks of Blairite councillors. Meanwhile, the community demonstrates outside the Town Hall and the trade unions organise strike ballots. The Labour left plays hardly any part in this activity, a far cry from the Islington 1993 nursery campaign. Worse, Labour Party members at the next council elections will be on the streets campaigning for a vote for the sitting Labour councillors, which means a vote for the ruling Labour–Tory coalition, which means, in effect, a vote for the Tories. The people of Hackney are being given no choice.

In the course of New Labour's next term in government, I expect the situation in Hackney to be repeated in different forms across Britain. The influence of millionaire donors will increase while trade unions are left to look after themselves. Should there be an economic downturn, Blair and Brown will undoubtedly expect working-class people to bear the burden. And I expect more Labour Party members to draw the conclusions that I have drawn.

Meanwhile, in the wide world outside the Labour Party, there are welcome signs of renewed political engagement. At every World Trade Organisation meeting, there are thousands of young (and not so young) people protesting outside, putting their bodies on the line in the struggle for a just world. More and more people are prepared to stand up and challenge corporate prerogatives. The movement for global social change exists, and is growing in strength, and I intend to continue playing my part in it.

I do not consider my years in the Labour Party as wasted years. I was proud to be part of a vital grassroots struggle for democratic reform. I respect the determination of my friends in the Grassroots Alliance to keep up the fight. But I believe that any further activity in the Labour Party would leave me at best silent and at worst complicit in promoting New Labour's ideology and power. So, after twenty-one years of active membership, I have left the Labour Party. I have certainly not left politics, the movement for social justice, or the search for socialism.

Appendix 1

Membership of the National Executive Committee

1998–1999

Ex officio

Tony Blair MP, Leader
Alan Donnelly MEP, Leader of the European Parliamentary
  Labour Party
John Prescott MP, Deputy Leader
Margaret Prosser, Treasurer

Trade union representatives (12 seats)

John Allen, AEEU
Brenda Etchells, AEEU and Chair of the Party
Mike Griffiths, GPMU
John Hannett, USDAW
Vernon Hince, RMT and Vice-Chair of the Party
Derek Hodgson, CWU
Diana Holland, TGWU
Maggie Jones, UNISON
Steve Pickering, GMB
Anne Picking, UNISON
Mary Turner, GMB
Margaret Wall, MSF

Constituency representatives (6 seats)

Michael Cashman
Liz Davies
Cathy Jamieson
Diana Jeuda
Mark Seddon
Pete Willsman

*Parliamentary and European Parliamentary Labour Party
representatives (3 seats)*

Anne Begg MP
Pauline Green MEP
Clive Soley MP

Labour councillor representatives (2 seats)

Sir Jeremy Beecham
Sally Powell

Government representatives (3 seats)

Hilary Armstrong MP
Ian McCartney MP
Mo Mowlam MP

Socialist societies (1 seat)

Dianne Hayter

Young Labour (1 seat)

Sarah Ward (replaced in July 1999 by Claire McCarthy)

1999–2000

Ex officio

Tony Blair MP, Leader
Alan Donnelly MEP, Leader of European Parliament Labour Party
(replaced January 2000 by Simon Murphy MEP)
John Prescott MP, Deputy Leader
Margaret Prosser, Treasurer

Trade union representatives (12 seats)

John Gibbins, AEEU
Mike Griffiths, GPMU
John Hannett, USDAW
Vernon Hince, RMT and Chair of the Party
Derek Hodgson, CWU
Diana Holland, TGWU
Maggie Jones, UNISON and Vice-Chair of the Party
Steve Pickering, GMB
Anne Picking, UNISON
Cath Speight AEEU
Mary Turner, GMB
Margaret Wall, MSF

Constituency representatives (6 seats)

Michael Cashman
Liz Davies
Diana Jeuda
Lord Tom Sawyer
Mark Seddon
Christine Shawcroft

Parliamentary and European Parliamentary Labour Party representatives (3 seats)

Helen Jackson MP
Dennis Skinner MP
Clive Soley MP

Labour councillor representatives (2 seats)

Sir Jeremy Beecham
Sally Powell

Government representatives (3 seats)

Hilary Armstrong MP
Ian McCartney MP
Mo Mowlam MP

Socialist societies (1 seat)

Dianne Hayter

Young Labour (1 seat)

Claire McCarthy

Margaret McDonagh attends all meetings as the Labour Party's General Secretary.

Motion and submission on the Labour Party's financial relations

Motion submitted to the NEC in January 1999 on conducting a review of Party sponsorship (no vote allowed; motion remitted to "review")

"The NEC believes that the Labour government and the Labour Party must not only be but be seen to be independent of all special interests, including commercial interests.

The NEC therefore resolves to establish a sub-committee to:

1. Review current party policy on sponsorship, advertising and exhibiting at Party conference and other party activities
2. Recommend to the full NEC criteria for future sponsorship, advertising and exhibiting that reflect:
   a. the Party's financial requirements;
   b. the need for the Labour Government to appear independent of special interests;
   c. Labour's values and its commitment to the needs of the many, not the few."

Submission to the Review on the Financial Relations of the Party from Liz Davies, NEC member
(submitted June 1999)

Introduction

None of us needs to be reminded of the sensitivity surrounding any major political party's large-scale fund-raising. The reasons for that sensitivity are obvious, particularly when the party is in government. Most corporate institutions are not known for their philanthropic spirit. The general assumption, from the press, the public and Party members, is that corporate donations to or sponsorship of the Party are intended to produce some benefit for the corporation involved. Inevitably, and not without reason, the public views the relationships between political parties and private corporations with some scepticism. Unless the Party embraces and publicises clear and unambiguous guidelines to govern its relations with companies, it will not be able to allay that scepticism.

Sponsorship – the current position

According to the Party's 1998 Annual Report, presented to 1998 Conference, "the Labour Party regards sponsorship as a commercial transaction wholly different from political donations". However, the Neill Committee explicitly includes sponsorship within its definition of political donations from companies, thus recognising that sponsorship is more than a straightforward commercial transaction. In what follows, I have considered sponsorship and donations together, as I believe the Party must do if it is to retain credibility.

Conflicts of interest

We must avoid any financial link which generates a potential conflict between the Party's financial interests and the government's duty to take decisions in the public interest.

In this regard, it is important to stress that the issue is not whether or not any particular donations or sponsorships actually have or have not influenced government decisions or Party policies, but whether they are *perceived* to have the potential to do so. It is vital that the public have total confidence that Party and government policies are formulated exclusively in the public interest. We must therefore ensure not only that there is no actual conflict of interest, but also that there is *seen to be* no conflict of interest.

The dangers to the Party of any perceived compromise on these questions have been brought home by several events since the last general election. The first was the relaxation on the ban on tobacco advertising in motor-racing followed by the Party's return of Bernie Ecclestone's donation. Another was a front-page story in the *Daily Mail* on 6 February 1999 which read "Labour's links to gene foods" and revealed that Novartis, a leading manufacturer of GM foods, had sponsored the Party. The revelation came out at the same time as the government was considering whether to ban GM foods.

Disclosure

Disclosure of corporate sponsors and donors has gone some way to ensuring that the Party's relations with companies are seen to be above board. The Party publishes a list of all organisations whose sponsorship of Party events or activities exceeds £5,000. The list contained in the 1998 Annual Report is of those organisations which sponsored events in 1997.

However, there is a need for a further step in openness and transparency. The Party should publish the specific amounts of donations or sponsorships over £5,000. Clearly, there is a difference between £5,000 and £50,000 or £100,000 or more, and the public will remain suspicious of a partial disclosure that appears to evade those differences in scale. This would be no more than already occurs with affiliated trade unions, whose fees to the Party are published in detail.

Ethical concerns

Guidelines exist in a document headed "donations to the Labour Party". Those guidelines apply to sponsorship as well as to donations. The Party undertakes disclosure of donations in excess of £5,000 per annum, and not to accept foreign-sourced donations. There is a general caveat: "The Labour Party may decide not to accept a donation offered for whatever reason." There is also a reference to principles which govern whether or not an offer of sponsorship is acceptable: "The Labour Party will not accept donations from companies the activities of which are inconsistent with the principles of the Labour Party." However, no criteria are stipulated according to which such donations or sponsorship might be deemed "inconsistent with the principles of the Labour Party" and therefore unacceptable. In the absence of such criteria, whether or not a particular donation or sponsorship arrangement is acceptable is left entirely to the judgement of the members of the Finance Sub-committee of the NEC on a case-by-case basis. Those individuals are therefore required to assess the acceptability of a donation or sponsorship without assistance by way of guidelines or agreed precedents, and, it seems, in the absence of detailed information on the company concerned. That is a very heavy burden and must give rise to concerns about inconsistent or arbitrary decision-making.

The publication of guidelines spelling out which types of company activity are not in accordance with the principles of the Party would assist in ensuring that the Party's financial dealings retain the confidence of Party members and the public. It would also help secure the Party's position in the public eye as a champion of a consistent set of moral and social values, and an enemy of special interests.

Specific cases: causes for concern

In the absence of any defined guidelines, the list of 1997 sponsors includes some disturbing entries. Two separate causes for concern can be identified. The first is those companies whose activities are unlikely to be considered "ethical" by Party members or sections of the public. The second is those companies which stand to benefit from specific government decisions, and whose financial contributions might be viewed as generating a conflict of interests. Some companies appear to fall into both camps. The lists below are not exhaustive, and are intended only as examples which might cause concern.

1. Companies whose activities may be considered not in accord with the Party's aims and values

Raytheon Systems Ltd. – one of the world's three largest arms manufacturers, it makes Tomahawk, Patriot, Hawk, Sidewinder and Stinger missiles. It supplies arms to Saudi Arabia, Malaysia, Singapore, Brunei, Indonesia and Thailand. It is based in the USA (and should therefore be ineligible as a sponsor even under the current guidelines) and has been found to be in breach of American labour law on a number of occasions.

Enron Europe Ltd. – this is a subsidiary of the American power firm Enron (and again should be ineligible as a sponsor by the current guidelines). The parent firm is the largest power corporation in the Indian subcontinent. It has been the subject of a report by Amnesty International condemning its human rights abuses. Amnesty reports that in 1997 local police arrived at a village near Bombay, outside of which Enron has built the subcontinent's largest power plant. The villagers had protested at destruction of their fisheries and their coconut and mango trees. The police arrived when the men were fishing and turned their batons on women and children, beating them and imprisoning hundreds of women. Amnesty reported that Enron security staff were involved and said that the police had been bought by the company for that operation.

British American Financial Services – now a separate company, but formerly controlled by British American Tobacco. Again, it appears ineligible under the current guidelines.

Novartis Pharmaceuticals UK Ltd. – associated with the Swiss company Novartis (and therefore presumably ineligible under the current guidelines). The Swiss company is one of the world's giants in GM food development.

2. *Companies whose sponsorship raises potential conflicts of interest*

Raytheon – Recently awarded a \$100 million contract by the Ministry of Defence.

Novartis – financial interest in the government's decision on banning or regulating GM foods.

Enron – bidding for Wessex Water.

Jarvis plc – not contained in the list of 1997 sponsors, but sponsored receptions and fringe meetings for councillors at 1998 Conference, currently bidding for PFI contracts in secondary schools.

Onyx UK – also a sponsor of fringe meetings and receptions for councillors at 1998 Conference, and a leading contractor for local government refuse-collection services.

Proposed guidelines

Once guidelines are in place, Party officials will be able to ascertain from public records whether there is any reason to believe particular companies are in breach of them, and to present information and advice to the members of the Finance Sub-committee, who would then be able to reach informed and consistent decisions.

Obviously, the formulation of guidelines would require research, deliberation and consultation. As a contribution to that process, I would offer the following as an initial proposal:

1. Conflicts of principle

The Party will not accept sponsorship or donations from companies the activities of which are inconsistent with the principles of the Labour Party. In particular, the Party will not accept sponsorship or donations from companies which sell or manufacture arms, which have engaged in practices that have been condemned as human rights abuses by Amnesty or other reputable international organisations, which sell or produce tobacco, which violate agreed environmental standards, or which have a practice of employing child labour. The Party will also not accept sponsorship or donations from any company which has been found liable for breaches of employment or labour law, or any law regulating company standards or standards for financial trading.

2. Potential conflicts of interest

The Party will not accept sponsorship or donations from companies which are bidding, or propose to bid in the eighteen months following the proposed event, for contracts from local or central government. The Party will not accept sponsorship or donations from companies whose activities are the subject of proposals for government regulation.

Financial impact of ethical standards

"Events and sponsorship" income comprises some 10 per cent of the Party's revenue. The published list does not specify the amounts contributed by individual companies. However, it seems unlikely that the amounts contributed by the companies to which an objection might be made are in any way essential to the Party's financial well-being. In addition, any assessment of the value to the Party of these contributions must also take into account the adverse publicity that is generated by the Party's association with these companies, and the potential loss of membership and support that can result.

Conclusion

Over the last twenty years, ethical investment campaigns have shown that it is possible for individuals and institutions to combine their financial objectives with their commitment to social concerns, such as social justice, economic development, peace or a healthy environment. The most high-profile example was the campaign to disinvest from apartheid, a cause taken up by many Labour local authorities, as well as individuals. Of course, there is a difference; the Labour Party is a receiver of, rather than an investor in, corporate money. However, there can be no denying that donations or sponsorships establish a financial tie between the Party and the donors and sponsors, and this tie is a public association, and will inevitably be construed by some as a mutual endorsement. To retain the confidence of the public and its own membership, the Party should require ethical standards from the companies from which it receives money; it should dissociate itself from companies which do not meet such standards; and it should ensure that no sponsorship or donation can be construed as having an undemocratic influence on government decision-making.

By establishing and sustaining the highest possible ethical standards for our own financial conduct, the Labour Party has the chance to challenge the widespread cynicism about democratic politics which is the greatest enemy of our shared hopes for the future.

Appendix 3

Dossier of complaints from Glenda Jackson and Ken Livingstone, submitted on 29 December 1999 to Unity Security Balloting Ltd

1. Membership lists were passed by Head Office directly to Dobson's campaign;
2. Party resources were used in support of Dobson to expedite quicker production of the membership list;
3. Party resources were used in support of Dobson in that facilities for telephone canvassing were made available by Mitcham and Morden Labour Party free of charge (whose MP is Siobhain McDonagh, sister of Margaret; both Siobhain and Margaret are members of Mitcham & Morden CLP);
4. That the recording of votes in the MPs' section was in contravention of the rules requiring a secret ballot;
5. That there was inconsistency, and therefore procedural unfairness, in the conduct of the ballot for the trade union section – Party members up to 15 months in arrears could vote, but the trade unions had to be affiliated by 31 December 1998;
6. Procedural unfairness in charging for the members' mailing provided by Millbank – since Dobson already had the membership list, he had no need to use the facility of two mailings provided by Millbank. Jackson and Livingstone (not having the lists) had to use the mailings and were charged £6,000 each;

7. That spending limits were being flexibly interpreted so that Dobson could spend in excess of the apparent limit of £62,750 (£1 per London Party member);

8. Procedural inconsistency in how votes would be cast in the trade union and socialist societies section: the rules prohibited trade unions from apportioning their votes, but some had indicated that they would split their votes;

9. Procedural inconsistency in that trade unions were not required to ballot their members, and therefore there was inconsistency between those who chose to ballot and those who did not;

10. Procedural inconsistency in that the selection of the candidate for Mayor was by an electoral college, whereas the selection of candidates for the GLA was by one member, one vote – the dossier recommended one member, one vote in both contests.

Index